50 ESSENTI
TE

For Michèle

50 ESSENTIAL MANAGEMENT TECHNIQUES

Michael Ward

Gower

Published 1995 in hardback by Gower Publishing Limited
Reprinted 1996

Paperback edition published 1998 by
Gower Publishing Limited
Gower House
Croft Road
Aldershot
Hampshire GU11 3HR
England

Gower
Old Post Road
Brookfield
Vermont 05036
USA

British Library Cataloguing in Publication Data

Ward, Michael
    50 Essential Management Techniques
    I. Title
    658

    ISBN 0–566–07532–6 (Hbk)
        0–566–08164–4 (Pbk)

Library of Congress Cataloguing-in-Publication Data

Ward, Michael.
    50 essential management techniques / Michael Ward.
        p.   cm.
    ISBN 0–566–07532–6
    1. Industrial management. 2. Strategic planning. I. Title.
    II. Title: Fifty essential management techniques.
    HD31.W32   1995
    658.4–dc20
                                                    94–44974
                                                    CIP

Typeset in Palatino by Raven Typesetters, Chester and printed in the United Kingdom at the University Press, Cambridge

Contents

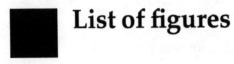

List of figures

List of tables

■ Preface

It is a truism that managers do not read. Certainly they do not read as much as they would like to read. In their defence, they cite the wearying, mind and body numbing tyranny of work; staying ahead of – or even in – the game requires a great deal of hard work. Privately, and sometimes publicly, many managers accept that they are not nearly as effective as they would like to be or feel they should be. But what can they do? Time, after all, is not on their side. Although management education has improved enormously in recent years, I often detect more than a faint disillusionment with it. 'Management education is all very well,' practising managers tell me, 'but it's not true to life. Compared to managerial life, it's very often pat. Managerial life is messy.'

Perhaps more than most management educationalists, I acknowledge that managerial life is indeed messy. For my first seven years in business, I received not one jot of management training or development. Worse, I was prey to the extreme loneliness of those running their own business. I was the boss; there was no-one with whom I could freely talk. Looking back, those seven years were scary. It was real 'seat of the pants' stuff. But, somehow, I survived and indeed thrived.

Particular memories stay in my mind and will probably always remain. I remember buying a cleaning firm and finding, to my horror after a few days, that the pricing structure was impossibly inconsistent. Over the years my predecessor had seemingly done many favours for many people. The prices were a joke. When I tackled him he suggested increasing them by about 5 per cent. I knew that if I didn't increase by 30 per cent, I would be out of business in two months. As it happened, this was in the middle of a recession!

All alone and with icy sweat on my brow, I sat down and reviewed my options. If I did nothing, I would go out of business. Therefore I had to increase prices. But 30 per cent? What percentage of customers would I lose? On the back of the proverbial envelope I started to do some sums. I'd never heard of 'what if's', but that's what I was doing – what iffing. I'd never heard of the price elasticity of demand (see Managing pricing) but that's what I was using. It occurred to me that losing customers would gain me time to win other, hopefully more lucrative, customers. So there was a benefit of sorts, although I wouldn't have described it as an opportunity benefit (see Managing decisions).

I survived. Prices went up by 30 per cent (much more in certain cases). I probably lost about 10 per cent of my customers. I devised what I didn't then realize was a standard costing system, so that there was internal consistency in the prices. Thus, when one customer complained that they were being charged unfairly vis-à-vis another customer, I could open my 'black book' and show them, chapter and verse, how both prices were derived from a standard system. This settled complaints. Customers didn't like it but they accepted it. I continued to give what I considered was good value but prices continued to go up. In fact, two years later, they had increased by about 120 per cent overall, I had lost about 35 per cent of my customers and I sold the business for more than twice what I had paid for it. Despite my well meaning advice, the new owner ran it into the ground – through sheer mismanagement. I used the money to send myself to business school.

Business school – at the ripe old age of thirty – was a revelation as well as a severe culture shock. I was hungry for concepts, instruments, techniques which I could use to practical advantage. Like many others, I realized that the teaching was rather pat but I didn't care. This was an opportunity to get out of the 'seat of the pants' mire before it claimed me. With this spirit of necessary pragmatism, it was only much later that I started to realize the true value of the concepts which are embedded in techniques. Without concepts, we are trapped in our experience, unable to stand outside it and learn from it. The behavioural learning cycle (see Managing learning), is pivotal because it is a technique which shows us how to use concepts to learn from experience. Otherwise, sooner or later, we are doomed. As Santayana memorably wrote, 'Those who do not learn from history are condemned to repeat it.'

The years went by. I used management concepts for practical advantage and I used them, more and more in my work as a management consultant, to help my clients reframe their experiences and structure their thinking – as Emile Ratón and Michèle do in 'Managing decisions'.

Another memory – not of a client but a colleague, Richard, to whom I then functioned unofficially as an internal consultant. I remember sitting down one afternoon with Richard and drawing concept after concept to aid him in his thinking. Richard, an able senior manager, looked at me after about the fifth concept and asked, point blank, 'How do you know about these things?' Some of the concepts I'd picked up at business school or from other sources, some I had created myself. But there had been a time, for instance in the cleaning business, when I hadn't known about the concepts which now came to me so easily and which seemed so alien yet so helpful to Richard – a man of undoubted ability. That afternoon, long ago, the idea for this book was born. It would be a book of management concepts – practical techniques – which people could use to learn from their experience and to gain tangible benefits. The concepts wouldn't be accompanied by pat case studies; they would be stories, culled mainly from my own experience, which would, very often, be fully as messy as genuine management experience is. They would be true to life.

So that is how this book came into being. If you have a specific problem such as 'How do I analyse my organization?' look it up in the relevant section – 'Managing strategy'. Alternatively, if you want to know 'How can I manage conflict?', look it up in the relevant section – 'Managing people'. Each entry will introduce the technique, explain how it works and illustrate it with a management 'story' – I hesitate to use the dread term 'case study'! By then, you should have a fair idea of what to do. Where possible, I have provided references; where I've developed a concept myself, there are none – although I make no claims of ownership. We continually invent – and re-invent – each other's work. If someone feels that I have abused or misinterpreted their favourite technique, then I apologize. But techniques can be used in different ways. What is right for me may not be right for you. Feel free to use these techniques in different ways and don't be afraid to create your own. Always work with what works best for you.

A plea for tolerance. Experienced managers will hoot with laughter at finding balance sheets, profit and loss accounts and SWOT analyses in this book. Doesn't everyone know about these? No – I'm afraid they don't. Many otherwise capable managers are petrified by finance; if this book helps them become a little less petrified, then it will have served them well. And one day when crisis strikes, you will be grateful that you read about the recovery cycle (Managing yourself). Besides, did anybody know about the knowledge grid (Managing learning) or Zipf's Law (Managing numbers)? And doesn't everyone need to know what even your best friend won't tell you – the Johari Window (Managing people)?

I don't think there's much more to say. This book is for you. Use it. As in my previous book *Why Your Corporate Culture Change Isn't Working ... And What To Do About It*, I have tried to elicit how it feels out there. Management can be scary; and it can be fun. It can give us terrible moments and it can give us times of immense fulfilment. Either way we learn. Good luck to you with your learning.

Michael Ward

PART I

Managing strategy

■ 1

The open system

■ *How to understand your business environment*

Whereas the closed system (see Managing operations. The closed system) looks at an organization in terms of its internal operations, the open system looks at an organization in terms of its relationships with outside influences. In organizations there is a perennial management temptation to become so involved in the day to day running of operations that attention becomes focused exclusively on the internal, to the detriment of the external. Often this tendency is augmented by poor time management (see Chapter 41 The priority grid).

The concept of a open system implies that organizations and individuals can interact with a potentially limitless horde of other organizations and individuals. Such interactions may present opportunities, threats or both. If these interactions are not controlled or, worse still, if key players are not identified early enough, then there may not be time for an organization to change its strengths and weaknesses in time to react to, for example, emergent competition or a takeover bid.

Corporate strategy is often treated as a black art. I think of

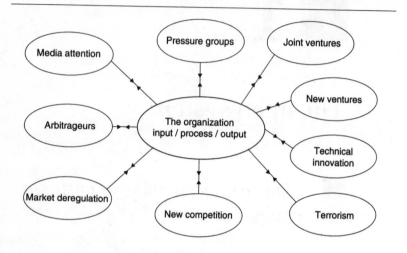

FIGURE 1.1 THE OPEN SYSTEM

strategy as a fog lamp in a moving car. The better the lamp, the further its light extends, the more it shows (of the open system), the less the chance of bumping into something hidden in the fog and the greater the chance of arriving at your original goal. Skill at corporate strategy can never guarantee success, but it will markedly decrease the probability of failure.

How to understand your business environment through the open system

At a strategy workshop with the directors of a chemical company, I began by explaining the principles of open and closed systems. The directors had previously admitted that they were far too much 'hands on' in the business. This was partly due to the management structure not working as it should; it was also partly due to the directors working more as operational department heads than as company directors. I pointed out that poor time management stressed urgency rather than importance, and that we were going to spend time looking at the vital issue of how their company stood in the outside world of the open system.

I asked the directors to brainstorm key outside influences and suggested a few myself. I then asked them to mark the influences as positive or negative. This proved quite difficult at times. For instance, achieving the quality standard BS 5750/ISO 9000 was seen both as negative (losing custom if they did not have it in place by the year end) and as positive (helping people to work in a more disciplined fashion). I then asked the directors to assign a score from 0 to 10 for impor-

---

TABLE 1.1 POSITIVE AND NEGATIVE INFLUENCES

Positive

Mergers and acquisitions	A chance to take over a competitor.
Joint ventures	A chance of a joint venture with a competitor.
Technical innovation	A prospect of a new, much more cost-effective refining method.
Market penetration	A chance to increase market share through reduced unit costs.

Negative

Quality	Losing custom through not getting the quality standard implemented in time.
Demographics	The plant was situated in a part of the country where key skills were in ever decreasing supply.
Legislation	Wading through a mass of EU directives seemed to be taking up an ever increasing amount of senior management time while apparently adding little of value to the business.
Media attention	The directors felt that their industry was continually being made a scapegoat by the media, with adverse effects on the workforce, customers, suppliers and contractors.

---

tance and for urgency for each influence. (On this basis, the negative score for BS 5750 was much higher than the positive score, so it was viewed as negative overall.) We identifiedpositives and negatives such as those shown in Table 1.1.

We now knew what were the key elements of the environment to which we would have to pay close attention. Obviously our effort was very much a first pass – but at least we had started to examine our environment in a systematic fashion.

Reference

Ward, Michael (1994), *Why Your Corporate Culture Change Isn't Working ... And What To Do About It*, Aldershot: Gower Publishing Ltd.

 **2**

SWOT analysis

■ *How to analyse your organization*

The SWOT analysis views an organization in terms of four attributes – Strengths, Weaknesses, Opportunities and Threats. It is an acronym derived from the first letters of each.

Strengths: what is the organization good at? What is its distinctive competence? Does it have a unique selling proposition (USP), vis-à-vis its competitors? Does it have advantages of situation, of market share, of public acclaim? Strengths might be a highly trained workforce, possession of relevant technical expertise, a commercially advantageous lease, protected patents.

Weaknesses: what is the organization bad at? Are its skills outdated? Is it forced to operate at a disadvantage relative to its competitors? Is it vulnerable in some way? Typical weaknesses might be ageing plant and equipment, restrictive work practices, a poorly trained workforce, obsolete technology.

Opportunities: what opportunities exist in the environment? Are there new markets opening up? Is there a possibility of a boom in demand? Might improved macroeconomic factors help trading? Would restructuring of grant agencies herald more generous relocation grants? Could exchange rate fluctuation or decreased interest rates give a competitive edge?

Threats: what threats might exist in the environment? Might the economy go into recession? Will overseas markets put up restrictive barriers? Is the industry contracting? Is there less potential for diversification? Is the organization under increasing threat from vandalism, crime, even terrorism?

How to analyse your organization using the SWOT analysis

In my strategy workshop with the directors of the chemical company (see 1 The open system), we began by considering open and closed systems. We then went on to brainstorm and systematically rank positive and negative external influences such as:

Positive: mergers and acquisitions, joint ventures, technical innovation and market penetration.
Negative: quality, demographics, legislation, media attention.

I then suggested making a SWOT analysis of the company. Whereas open and closed systems had been unfamiliar to the directors, all of them were familiar with SWOT analyses. It took a few minutes for people to realize.

'You crafty so and so,' chuckled Roger, the sales director. 'You've deliberately engineered this.' He turned to his fellow directors. 'What are the positive and negative influences from the open system but opportunities and threats?'

'That's right,' I replied, 'opportunities and threats belong to the open system whereas strengths and weaknesses belong to the closed system. Organizations exist in a state of dynamic balance between open and closed systems. If an opportunity such as your proposed joint venture is matched with a strength such as high operational flexibility, the opportunity will probably stand a much greater chance of working than if it is matched with a weakness such as restrictive practices. Alternatively, if a threat such as lost trade through lack of a quality standard is matched with a weakness such as poor ability to manage change, it's potentially very harmful; whereas if the threat is matched by a strength, such as good ability to manage change, it is potentially far less harmful. The trick is to keep changing internally so that strengths can be developed to minimize threats and maximize opportunities. Weaknesses will always exist; constant effort must be made to overcome them. And constant vigilance must be exercised over the open system; it is changing all the time and, if we do not correspondingly change, we will become extinct. Strengths such as patent protection can develop weaknesses such as corporate complacency; whereas weaknesses such as poor procurement can be made to yield both benefits and strengths. It's a never ending process.'

'Now, let's finish off the SWOT analysis by listing and ranking our strengths and weaknesses and seeing how well they match the opportunities and threats. The better the fit, the better the chances of continued success. The areas of poor fit will identify development needs for the organization. Strategy may start with divergent thought; it soon ends up with convergent action!'

Reference
Armstrong, M. (1986), *A Handbook of Management Techniques*, London: Kogan Page Ltd.

■ 3

Stakeholder/role set analysis

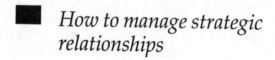

■ *How to manage strategic relationships*

Stakeholder analysis charts the open system in terms of people, organizations and domains which are relevant to a particular organization, or person. Although the ultimate open system is the entire universe, the emphasis is on relevance in terms of opportunities and threats.

Stakeholder domains: these might be mergers and acquisitions, quality, information technology (IT) or new product development. Whether as opportunities or threats, these are areas of crucial importance to the organization.

Stakeholder organizations: these might be suppliers, customers, competitors, collaborators in joint ventures, providers of funds, government departments, grant bodies, etc.

Individual stakeholders: these might be investment analysts, chief executives, journalists, lobbyists, etc.

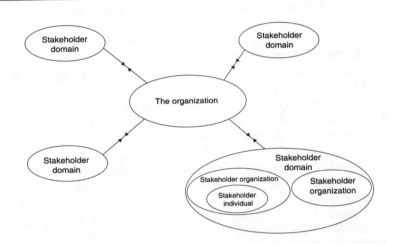

FIGURE 3.1 STAKEHOLDER/ROLE SET ANALYSIS

Role set: having identified the key stakeholders by domain, organization and individual, role set considers the relationships between such key stakeholders and ourselves/each other. Managing the open system means managing relationships with key stakeholders in terms of role – i.e. mutual expectation. By following a systematic process of stakeholder/role set analysis, the nature of such mutual expectation will become much more clear.

How to manage strategic relationships through stakeholder/role set analysis

In my workshop with the directors of the chemical company (see 2 The SWOT analysis), we went from analysing the open system in terms of opportunities and threats to analysing the closed system in terms of strengths and weaknesses. We now had a complete SWOT analysis and faced the task of improving strengths to exploit opportunities and minimize threats while acting to nullify weaknesses. My clients were able and pragmatic people who were used to analysing problems into their elements and resolutely attacking them. It soon became apparent, however, that they were far less used to managing relationships with representatives of outside bodies, particularly antagonistic ones. To this end, I asked them to provide a stakeholder analysis of threats. Two domains identified were environmental (the company had pollution problems) and the City (the company had recently acquired PLC status). The environmental domain included organizations in environmental, political and media areas while the City domain included organizations in the institutional, financial and media areas. Within each domain were key stakeholder organizations and individuals.

'Like it or not,' I said, 'we live in a complex world with a great deal of power to influence us. We have charted the threats segment of the open system into two domains and further charted those domains in terms of constituent organizations and people. Whatever your strategic intent, you have to conduct relationships with these people, which result in mutually advantageous roles being negotiated and mutually accceptable outcomes realized. Let's start by writing down for each stakeholder domain, organization and person what are our expectations of them and what we think are their expectations of us.

Having done that, we identified potential and actual areas of conflict which needed resolving (for instance with environmentalist groups) and opportunity (for instance with an investment group). We now had a plan for action. The environment was much less amorphous than before. Our strategic lamp was cutting a swathe through what had previously been impenetrable fog.

Reference
Handy, Charles (1976), *Understanding Organizations*, Penguin Books Ltd.

PART II

Managing marketing

■ 4

The product life cycle

■ *How to assess the marketability of your product*

The product life cycle shows that a product's market life, i.e. the time that people will want to buy it, has at least four phases.

Phase 1 is an exploratory innovative phase. The product is being invented and/or developed. Very few people however have actually bought it. Usually the product is prohibitively expensive – because the development costs have to be recouped. An example of a phase 1 product would be video recorders in the 1960s. Some people did have them!

Phase 2 represents a boom expansion in demand. Ownership of the product is increasing. Previously ownership of the product was a minority interest; now mass markets are developing. An example of a phase 2 product would be videos in the 1980s.

Phase 3 represents market saturation. Many people now have the product. Producing the product is profitable because the

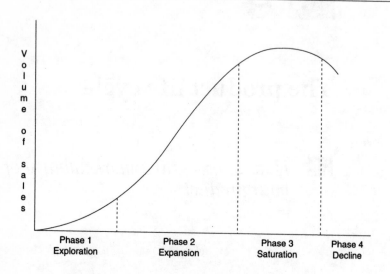

| Phase 1 | Phase 2 | Phase 3 | Phase 4 |
| Exploration | Expansion | Saturation | Decline |

FIGURE 4.1 THE PRODUCT LIFE CYCLE

original development costs have been absorbed. However, competitors are moving into the market. Marketing skills are paramount. An example of a phase 3 product is cornflakes – need you ask whose?

Phase 4 is a phase of decline. The market is saturated and has become refined. Few people want this product any more. The product is consequently relatively very cheap. An example of a phase 4 product is black and white television in the 1990s.

How to assess the marketability of your product using the product life cycle

James Hinton belonged to the fifth generation of the Hinton family to be involved in the family business. Hinton diaries had been famous for decades. George Bernard Shaw had extolled the virtues of Hinton diaries as had Winston Churchill. One hundred and fifty years after George Hinton had set up business in Leeds, his eponymous diaries were still being bought in their millions. This was of scant consolation to James, who was being squeezed hard by rising manufacturing costs and fierce competition.

A board meeting was convened to discuss what should be done. Older members of the Hinton family were appalled to hear young Jeremy Hinton blithely declare, 'Diaries are finished; they are a thing of the past. I wouldn't be seen dead using one and nor would anyone I know. This is what we've got to get into,' he insisted, pulling a personal organizer out of his jacket pocket and brandishing it.

At a subsequent strategy workshop, a management consultant asked the board to place their diaries on the product life cycle curve. After some discussion they placed them in phase 3 – market saturation. They were then asked to place personal organizers on the same curve. This time they unhesitatingly chose phase 1. 'If you go down the personal organizer route,' the consultant pointed out, 'you are in phase 1 – high development costs in technologies about which you know nothing, and a tiny emergent market. If you stay with the diaries you have very considerable markets – people all over the world know and love Hinton diaries. The task then becomes to make those markets pay. Better manufacturing will cut your unit costs and slicker marketing of the Hinton name will command a premium price. The result? Increased profitability, maintained dividends and revenues to support new product development. So,' he challenged them, 'which is it to be – the dangers of phase 1 or the known territory of phase 3?'

'Put like that,' Roderick Hinton acknowledged, 'there's no choice.' Even Jeremy nodded.

Reference
Kotler, P. (1983), *Principles of Marketing*, 2nd Edn., New York: Prentice-Hall Inc.

■ 5

The profit impact of market share

■ *How to chart your product's profitability cycle*

The profit impact of market share looks at four phases of a product's market share in terms of their profitability.

Phase 1 is where market share is low but increasing. Products here are known as 'problem children'. Like problem children in domestic life, they may consume a great deal of attention. Unlike problem children in domestic life, managements have to consider whether further effort is justified. Only a few problem children reach the next phase. An example of a problem child which failed to reach the next phase is Clive Sinclair's electric car – a concept well ahead of its time.

Phase 2 is where market share is high and growing fast – a marketeer's dream! Premium prices may be charged, the future looks rosy. The product almost seems to be selling itself; consequently, marketing skills may be less important. Products in this phase are known as 'stars', for example video cassette recorders in the late 1970s.

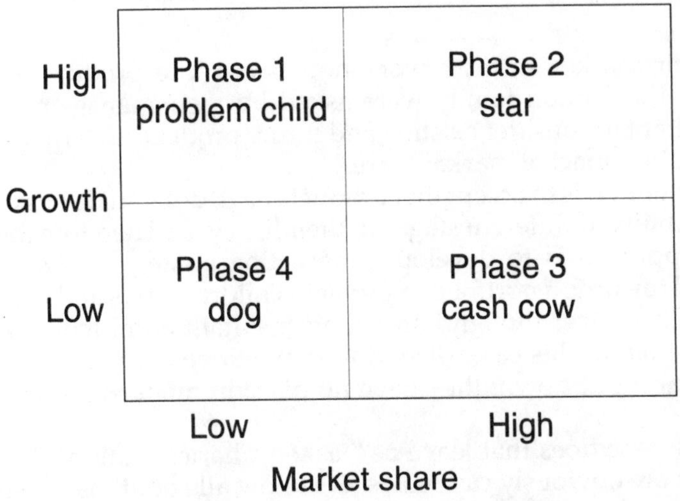

	Low	High
High Growth	Phase 1 problem child	Phase 2 star
Low	Phase 4 dog	Phase 3 cash cow

Low   High

Market share

FIGURE 5.1 THE PROFIT IMPACT OF MARKET SHARE

Phase 3 is where there is a declining share of a large market. Because development costs have long since been recouped, this can be a phase of immense profitability. But beware! Competitors will covet such profitability. Marketing skills are paramount. Products in phase 3 are known, aptly, as 'cash cows'. Such cash cows would be videos, camcorders and personal computers in the 1980s.

Phase 4 is where market size and share are in decline – truly a sad occurrence which may baffle the skills of the most experienced marketeer. Products in phase 3 are called 'dogs'. A typical dog is black-and-white television. I quite like it; nobody else seems to.

Phases 1, 2, 3 and 4 of the profit impact of market share broadly correspond to phases 1, 2, 3 and 4 of the product life cycle. The two concepts, although separate, complement each other well.

How to chart your product's profitability cycle using the profit impact of market share

At their market strategy workshop (see 4 The product life cycle), the Hinton family were asked by their management consultant to consider existing and future products in terms of the profit impact of market share.

'The notion is to accept that products have different levels of profitability at different stages in their life cycle. Therefore the best approach is to develop a marketing strategy which is geared towards a portfolio of problem children, stars and cash cows. Dog lover though I am,' the consultant admitted, 'I'm afraid that, in this case, dirty dogs have to be quickly recognized and put down; they have no place in modern marketing.'

'So where does that leave us?' asked Charles Hinton. 'The diaries are obviously cash cows. We know all about them. No matter what we do, sooner or later, they'll end up as dirty dogs. The address books seem like stars at the moment. The old range of cloth covered diaries were dogs; we eliminated them a couple of years ago. Problem children? I can't see any of them, I'm afraid.'

'The leather covered diaries are cash cows,' James Hinton agreed. 'What I don't think we've realized is the prospect of retaining them as cash cows by clever marketing. Look at bibles; they are still selling. I can't help feeling that those diaries have a lot of life left in them yet.'

'I agree,' the consultant concurred. 'Hinton's diaries have a long way to go. Now, with the address book, we possess a problem child which seems to have succeeded in becoming a star. But we need to develop more problem children, some of which will become stars, some won't. Although electronic organizers are too big a risk, in my opinion, what is to stop us having a look at the normal personal organizer market? After all, that's leather and paper also.

'The best way of looking at it is probably to consider ourselves skilled in designing, manufacturing and distributing luxury products in leather and paper – products which people use to record events, plan and organize themselves. There are many potential problem children – personal organizers, specialized diaries, document wallets, to name but three.

'We must build upon our core skills to develop a portfolio of problem children, stars and cash cows, and support each with relevant marketing expertise. We need eggs in several baskets. But no dogs, gentlemen – absolutely no dogs!'

Reference
Kotler, P. (1983), *Principles of Marketing*, 2nd Edn., New York: Prentice-Hall Inc.

■ 6

The market/product grid

■ *How to develop your marketing strategy*

The market/product grid considers the four possible combinations of market and product in terms of whether each is existing or new.

Quadrant 1: this is known territory – existing products in existing markets.

Quadrant 2: here we are introducing a new product into an existing market. We know about the market but we do not know how well the new product will be received. Thus the situation is more uncertain than it was in quadrant 1.

Quadrant 3: here we are introducing existing products into new markets. Again the situation is more uncertain than it was in quadrant 1. It is the converse of the situation in quadrant 2. We know about the product but we do not know about the market.

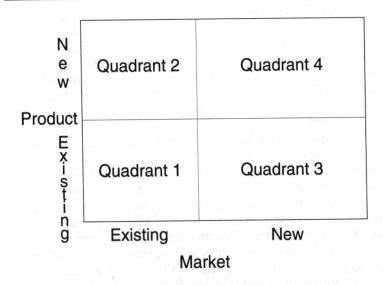

FIGURE 6.1 THE MARKET/PRODUCT GRID

Quadrant 4: here we are introducing new products into new markets. This is by far the most uncertain quadrant as not only do we face a learning curve with the products but we will also face a learning curve with the markets. Quadrant 4 is for the foolish and the brave!

How to develop your marketing strategy by using the market/product grid

During a marketing strategy workshop with the Hinton family (see 5 The profit impact of market share), the management consultant leading the workshop introduced the concept of the market/product grid. He explained the different quadrants and asked the various members of the Hinton family present to relate their products to the quadrant in which they felt they belonged.

'Well, our diaries are obviously an existing product in an existing market,' James Hinton observed. 'Our address books would be a new product in an existing market. They've done rather well,' he murmured. 'Jeremy's organizers sound like new products in new markets,' he continued with obvious distaste. 'What about existing products in new markets?' the consultant queried. 'Hmm ... put like that, you have a point,' James agreed.

'When people talk about mature markets they inevitably begin to think in terms of diversification,' the consultant pointed out. 'Almost always, people are tempted by diversification of product and market, i.e. quadrant 4, new product and new market. But product 4 is so dangerous – the uncertainty of the market is compounded by the uncertainty of the product. The irony is that moving into quadrant 4 is rarely necessary'.

'Hinton diaries are renowned the world over,' he continued. 'I've got one myself,' he admitted. 'I've owned a Hinton diary ever since I could afford one. But that's the rub. Look around us, gentlemen. With the exception of Jeremy, none of us is in the first flush of youth. If we continue to rely on existing markets, we will find ourselves selling diaries to fewer and fewer ageing people. Jeremy maintains that diaries are a thing of the past. I disagree. I think that people will be using paper diaries in 20 years' time when our present electronic organizers will be embarrassing technological dinosaurs. Our task is to convince people of Jeremy's generation that it's chic to own a Hinton diary – that the quality of the leather and paper is much more aesthetic than a soulless organizer. That will give us sales in quadrant 3, existing products in new markets. We can continue with developing other aesthetic products in leather and paper, such as address books, for quadrant 2, new products in existing markets. Obviously we must not neglect our mainstay, quadrant 1, existing products in existing markets. And if we must venture into quadrant 4, new products in new markets, why not Hinton's address books for cool dudes?' At this, everyone groaned. Even the noticeably discomfited Jeremy smiled wryly.

Reference
Ansoff, H.I. (1965), *Corporate Strategy*, New York: McGraw-
Hill Book Co.

■ 7

The four Ps

■ *How to manage tactical marketing*

The four Ps of marketing tactics are: 1. Product, 2. Price, 3. Promotion, 4. Place.

Product: are we marketing the right product to our target market? What is the demand for our product? How do we know that this demand exists? Why does this demand exist? What might cause this demand to change? Common sense might suggest a market for bikinis in the Bahamas and waterproofs in Wester Ross. But what about bikinis in Wester Ross and waterproofs in the Bahamas? Assume nothing. Find out.

Price: is our price right for our target market? Is it too high or too low? What is the likely price sensitivity of demand (see Part III Managing pricing)? What might be the effect of discounting and/or special offers? How will the target market view our product in terms of price? Relatively inexpensive vegetables may be positively viewed by women with a limited budget while inexpensive ballgowns may be negatively viewed by those same women. Or vice versa. Assume nothing.

Promotion: how will we let our target market know about our product? Word of mouth is simple and inexpensive – but is it enough? Television advertising for a home improvement service will reach many many people – but what proportion of these will constitute our target market? What are the respective merits of newspapers, billboards, trade journals, public relations, telemarketing or field sales? Which media/combinations are right for us?

Place: where should we be situated? Does it matter – and if so, why? Will our customers be coming to see us or will we be going to see them? How important is parking? What about other forms of access, for example Underground stations? What if the road is made one-way? How important is passing trade? The correct location for a supermarket may be very different to the correct location for an upmarket boutique.

How to manage tactical marketing: The four Ps

Dave and Joe were contemplating opening an outdoor equipment shop in Manchester. Both were active in the outdoors, fell running, climbing, skiing, canoeing and walking. Thus they knew their products well. They had begun in retailing several years previously by opening a small climbing shop in North Wales. From there, they had opened a similar shop in Derbyshire. The shop in Manchester would be their third. Although the marketing for the first two shops had been very much by 'gut feel' ('In each case, we knew the area and the clientele,' Dave admitted), with the move to Manchester they felt the need for a more professional marketing approach.

'There is certainly scope for another outdoor equipment shop in Manchester, 'Dave emphasized.' I keep bumping into people from Manchester at climbing walls. They tell me that they buy equipment in Altrincham and Sheffield. They should be buying it in Manchester.'

'That's true,' Joe agreed. 'I've had a look at the existing choice. Currently you can go to three shops, all of which stock basic climbing equipment. But none of them cater for serious climbers. And everybody knows how fussy serious climbers are.'

'There are a lot of active climbers in Manchester, and we can do some market research to find out how many and what the average yearly spend is,' Joe continued. 'I think we should specialize in high quality climbing equipment. I know the canoes sold well in Wales and the skis in Derbyshire. But Manchester already has a number of canoe and ski shops. We don't want to be competing with them; we can't profitably be all things to all people.'

After considerable discussion, Dave and Joe agreed to sell only mountaineering products, but to stock an extensive range for beginner and expert alike. 'That way, we can encourage beginners to become committed customers,' Joe stressed. 'We can charge premium, but not extortionate, prices for specialist gear but basic equipment must be relatively cheap. That takes care of product and price for the moment.'

Promotion was relatively easy – mountaineering journals for a general market and an opening party for anyone who cared to attend. 'That way, at least everyone will know where to find us,' Dave declared. 'It's not that simple, I'm afraid,' Joe replied. 'We have a choice of three locations. The first is near the city centre, which is convenient for office workers but very expensive and with no parking. The second is in a very rough area, very cheap and with ample parking. The third site is within walking distance of the centre, medium expense and limited parking.' In the end, the third site and the fourth P were chosen.

Reference
Kotler, P. (1980), *Principles of Marketing*, 2nd Edn., New York: Prentice-Hall Inc.

■ 8

Features and benefits

■ *How to sell the right things*

The distinction between features and benefits is fundamental to selling. Experienced salespeople have (or should have!) the distinction between features and benefits indelibly imprinted upon their minds. However, few people who are not sales professionals are aware of the distinction. The irony is that we are all salespeople in every aspect of our lives. The young girl heading for the cosmetics counter is getting ready to package the product, i.e. sell herself, both to her peers in terms of social acceptance and to those whom she finds sexually attractive. What is the young boy doing in asking for a date if not selling himself? The college lecturers, on their promotion stand in the middle of town, are blatantly selling themselves. The job applicant, the promotion seeker, the fundraiser, are all selling themselves. Each of us, in all aspects of our lives, both domestic and professional, is selling himself or herself. Managers, by the very nature of their vocation, must influence people to take certain courses of action. What is that if not selling? Every manager must learn to be a salesperson. Thus every manager needs to know about features and benefits.

Features relate to the technical nature of a product. The horn, the accelerator, the radiator and the clutch are all technical aspects of a car; none of these features, by themselves, will induce us to buy a car. Windows, doors, room size and elevation are all technical aspects of a house; none of these, by themselves, will induce us to buy a house. Features are merely neutral technical properties of a product or service.

Benefits are features of a product or service brought to life. Car model A is made in such a way that it is the safest car on the road to drive (benefit). The elevation of the house and the size of the windows give an unparalleled view over the bay (benefit). The thickness of the steak is a feature but the mouthwatering sizzle is undoubtedly a benefit. Benefits are what the product or service can **achieve** for the buyer.

Dynamic benefits are the benefits which the product or service can achieve for you **personally**. They relate directly to your, the buyer's, unique set of needs. Dynamic benefits might be the feeling of your long blonde hair blowing in the wind as you drive your new sports car, the joy you feel as you graduate from your course, the competitive advantage to your company in achieving an internationally recognized quality standard.

How to sell the right things by using features and benefits

Peter had joined a large organization as a technical specialist. Previously he had managed small departments, of no more than half-a-dozen people, all operating within his chosen specialism. As a result of a reorganization he found himself, to his horror, heading a department of some 80 people. Furthermore the department did fairly routine administrative work, unrelated to his specialism. Worse, it had a bad reputation in the parent organization. For years it had been used as a dumping ground for those – managers and managed alike – who had failed at other jobs in other parts of the organization. Perhaps, thought Peter ruefully, that was why he had ended up running it.

When I first encountered Peter, he was spending most of his time locked away in his office, understanding the technical aspects – such as they were – of his new operation. After considerable discussion he admitted that the technical aspects were relatively unimportant. He was at a complete loss as to how to turn the department around. After further discussion, we worked out a strategy to do just that. I had to intervene however when Peter attempted to send out a memo explaining the new strategy.

'It's no good doing that, Peter. People won't become committed to the new strategy just by reading about its features. They need to know about its benefits. And you are going to have to sell those benefits to them. So you're going to have to know what makes your people tick. It's dynamic benefits which matter – how this strategy will benefit your people in this department, right now.'

A most reluctant salesperson, Peter nevertheless had integrity and staying power. He started with selling to himself the primary benefit of the new strategy – a revitalized department, which people would take seriously. He sold himself the personal benefits of implementing the new strategy (personal development, experience of implementing change, a more impressive track record, the satisfaction of knowing that what he was doing was right). He sold everyone the benefits of a networked computer system (better communications, less drudgery). He sold people the benefit of a structure based on product groupings not functions (better customer service). He sold his managers the benefit of devolved power (better delegation). He sold the workforce the benefits of problem solving teams (personal development, an active say in the running of the business, the chance to kill off frustrating problems). Against all predictions, he sold the secretaries the benefits of controlling their own work flow (less disruption and stress). Against all odds, he sold senior management in the parent organization the benefit of an increased budget (work done more cost effectively in his department). Not bad going from a department full of unwanted personnel and a man who couldn't sell!

Reference
Bettger, F. (1990), *How I Raised Myself From Failure To Success In Selling*, London: Octopus Publishing Group.

PART III

Managing pricing

■ 9

The supply/demand curve

■ *How to manage demand*

The supply/demand curve is one of the great tenets of macro-economics. It considers the effect of price and volume upon two factors – demand (i.e. the number of products or services wanted by people) and supply (i.e. the number of products or services created and thereby made available).

At point A demand exceeds supply – there is not enough of the product to go round. Therefore the product attracts a premium price, for instance centre court tickets for a Wimbledon final.

At point B supply and demand are equal. What is made is sold, for instance bread in the shops. Pricing is keen. Markets are competitive.

At point C there is over-supply in the market, for instance the European car market in the early/mid 1990s. Discounting and special inducements will probably be the order of the day.

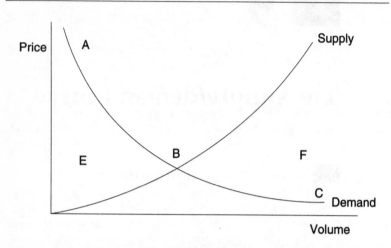

FIGURE 9.1 THE SUPPLY/DEMAND CURVE

Area E where demand exceeds supply, represents an area of lost sales. If the commodity were only available.... The market will shortly be crowded with new entrants ensuring that it is.

Area F represents sales which on a strict macroeconomic basis will not materialize. But, where there is a will, usually a way will be found.

How to manage demand by using the supply/demand curve

Jaime had discovered a new process which dramatically altered the hysteresis of rubber. In non-chemical terms, this made the rubber sticky. Thinking around for possible customers of sticky rubber, he came upon one outstanding group – rock climbers! Making the soles of climbing shoes out of stickier rubber gave increased friction advantages on many types of rock features, such as steep granite slabs.

Jaime sold his idea – and the accompanying patent – to a Spanish firm which manufactured climbing boots. They quickly realized that they had a unique opportunity to decimate the opposition.

The key members of the marketing team immediately met to discuss strategy and tactics. Even with patent protection, they estimated that they only had two years before their competitors were bringing similar models onto the market. They had to make the best of those two years; in so doing, they invoked the supply/demand curve. First, they worked out potential demand for their product. Worldwide, it was staggering. Every serious rock climber, no matter how conservative, would one day want a pair of sticky rubber boots.

Initially they chose premium pricing and marketing aimed at the élite. For most climbers, sticky rubber would confer a technical advantage which, while desirable, was not really essential. For the élite however, those operating at the cutting edge of contemporary standards, sticky rubber would probably be the determining factor in what was possible. Would they pay twice as much for a pair of rock boots?

The supply/demand curve suggested they might. And they did. With the élite usage of the sticky rubber boots came élite status. And so the non-élite began to buy them, still at premium prices. As the spectre of competition approached, it was decided to lower the prices and introduce more downmarket models to capture increased market share. By the time the first serious competition emerged, two years later as predicted, the secured revenues and market penetration were immense. The supply/demand relationship had been faithfully followed – to good effect.

Reference
Samuelson, P.A. (1992), *Economics*, 14th Edn., New York: McGraw-Hill.

■ 10

The price elasticity of demand

■ *How to manage pricing policy*

The price elasticity of demand considers the sensitivity of demand to price and increases or reductions in price. If the price of cornflakes went up by 15 per cent in the supermarket, it would probably raise a furore among shoppers. The same shoppers will, very often, unhesitatingly pay much more than 15 per cent over the odds for a luxury item or, more accurately, one which is deemed to have 'luxury' status. Conversely, dropping the price of a supposedly luxury item by 15 per cent may actually cause demand to fall, through a perception that the item is not so luxurious after all.

Cost-plus approaches to pricing (i.e. adding up your costs and adding on a 'reasonable' profit) are doomed to disaster in a free market. The only sensible approach to pricing is to determine what the market will bear and then ensure that you can control costs to give yourself a desired level of profit. The price elasticity of demand is a technique to investigate what the market will bear. The price/demand equation is as shown in Table 10.1.

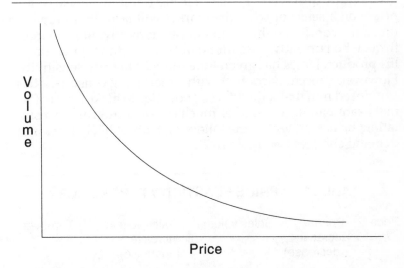

FIGURE 10.1 THE PRICE ELASTICITY OF DEMAND

TABLE 10.1 PRICE, VOLUME AND TURNOVER

Price × Volume = Turnover
P   ×   V   = PV

Through estimating changes in V due to changes in P, we can ascertain likely levels of turnover, i.e. answer the question as to whether we will gain or lose significant business.

How to manage pricing in terms of the price elasticity of demand

James produces a particular piece of climbing equipment,

priced at £10. Typically he sells 1 000 pieces per month. Thus, his monthly turnover is £10 000. He has traditionally based his prices on a sense of what the market will bear. From time to time, he considers the competition, typically much larger firms who currently pose minimal threat to the reputation of his product. James has given little thought to price sensitivity. However, a recent encounter with a marketing consultant has convinced him that it might be a good idea to make a more formal examination. Thus, after much consideration and consultation, he has drawn up the following table of likely price and demand changes (see Table 10.2).

TABLE 10.2 PRICE ELASTICITY IN PRACTICE

Price	Price increase (decrease)	Sales volume	Sales volume increase (decrease)	Turnover
£10	0%	1 000	0%	£10 000
£11	10%	850	(15%)	£ 9 350
£12	20%	800	(20%)	£ 9 600
£ 9	(10%)	1 200	20%	£10 800
£ 8	(20%)	1 300	30%	£10 400

It is obvious from Table 10.2 that James' product is fairly price sensitive. If he pushes prices up by 10 per cent, he loses 15 per cent custom, whereas if he pushes prices up another 10 per cent to 20 per cent, he only loses another 5 per cent, i.e. 20 per cent overall. Conversely, if he drops prices by 10 per cent, he gains 20 per cent custom, but if he drops them by a further 10 per cent he will only gain another 10 per cent custom; i.e. 30 per cent overall. If James wants to increase turnover, he should, on the evidence of these figures, decrease his prices by 10 per cent. Alternatively, he should increase his prices by 20 per cent. The latter may be the best solution for his profitability. All other solutions appear to fall short.

Of course, James must have an awareness of the strategic consequences of his actions. Increasing or decreasing prices will send out signals to his customers and competitors. He must also be heedful of these signs – and their possible consequences.

Reference
Samuelson, P.A. (1992), *Economics*, 14th Edn., New York: McGraw-Hill.

PART IV

Managing finance

■ 11

The balance sheet

■ *How to manage assets and liabilities*

The balance sheet is the prime description of the financial state of a business. Equally, it describes the financial situation of a non-profit making organization. It is, in a sense, a snapshot of a business. If a balance sheet were prepared a day or a week later, it would be somewhat different. However, the only way in which a business can report on the overall state of its financial affairs is to prepare a balance sheet, unfettered by the constraints of creative accounting.

Long term liabilities and fixed assets will not change from day to day. Current assets and liabilities will change. As assets can only be financed by liabilities, and as liabilities can only be spent on assets, it follows that the sum of the assets must be exactly equal to the sum of the liabilities. Thus a properly prepared balance sheet must balance.

TABLE 11.1 THE BALANCE SHEET

Liabilities	Assets
Long term liabilities	*Fixed assets*
Share capital	Land and buildings
Retained profits	Plant and machinery
Long-term loans	Office furniture/equipment
	Vehicles
Current liabilities	*Current assets*
Short-term loans	Material stocks
	Work in progress
Creditors	Finished goods stocks
Tax due	Debtors
Bank overdraft	Short-term investments
Dividends	Cash

How to manage assets and liabilities through the balance sheet

Mary, Simon and Robin had all worked for some time with a healthfood supplier in Leeds. Dissatisfied with his increasingly autocratic style and methods, they had resigned, determined to branch out on their own. Mary insisted that they make a start by learning something about finance. Simon was dubious.

'It's not as though Marcus knew anything about finance when he started out. He was repping for Marshalls and spotted a gap in the market. Simple as that.'

'I don't think we should necessarily be guided by what Marcus did and didn't do,' Mary tartly replied. 'Marcus survived three near financial crashes through his colossal ignorance of how to handle money. I don't want us to go down the same path.' 'Agreed,' Robin concurred.

So that was that. Thus, a week later, the threesome sat down for a one day workshop with Jenny, their new-found accountant. She began by building up a simple model of a balance sheet.

'The balance sheet is the financial portrait of a business. We must consider a business as a discrete entity. Even if all the liabilities were your own money, you would have to consider it money which you had lent to the business and which the business owed you. So, in trading terms, it would not be your own money; it would belong to the business.'

'The distinction between long-term and short-term seems sensible,' Robin agreed. 'What would you regard as long-term?' 'Oh, a year, at least,' Jenny told him. 'The point is that current assets and liabilities are changing all the time; fixed assets aren't. You're not going to buy or sell a factory overnight; nor should you be continually financing and refinancing your operation.'

'Is there any significance in the way you've listed the various liabilities and assets?' asked Mary.

'Yes,' Jenny replied. 'They are listed in increasing order of liquidity as you go down the page. For instance, if you needed ready money, for example to pay a pressing creditor, the fastest place to find it from would be cash from current assets. The next fastest place to find it would be from cashing in short-term investments, for instance shares.'

Simon frowned. 'Wouldn't you simply see the bank manager and increase your overdraft?'

'Increasing your overdraft would further increase your liabilities. Certainly, if you borrowed more money then it would appear as extra cash which could be used to pay off a creditor. But,' she looked at him levelly, 'it's robbing Peter to pay Paul.'

'Which is exactly what dear Marcus was so fond of doing,' Robin murmured. Mary looked at Jenny. 'And it's what we won't be doing,' she grimly assured them.

Reference
Reid, W. and Myddelton, D.R. (1992), *The Meaning Of Company Accounts*, 5th edition, Aldershot: Gower Publishing Ltd.

■ 12

The profit and loss account

■ *How to manage profit*

The profit and loss account, commonly known as the P&L, reveals the profitability or otherwise of an operation. It goes from the top line, the turnover, to the bottom line, the profit or loss. As seen in Table 12.1, there are different types of profit, such as gross profit, trading profit, net profit before tax and net profit. A business is the creation of people; thus, the policy on profitability must be decided by managers and/or shareholders. If, however, a business is regarded as a living entity, the aim is generally to increase the health of that entity by increasing the profit – the net profit, the true bottom line.

How to manage profit through the profit and loss account

Having dealt with the balance sheet at the finance workshop (see 11 The balance sheet), Jenny, Mary, Robin and Simon carried on to look at the P&L.

TABLE 12.1 THE PROFIT AND LOSS ACCOUNT

Turnover	£100 000	
Cost of sales	£ 64 000	
Gross profit	£ 36 000	
Distribution costs	£ 12 000	
Administration costs	£ 13 000	
	£ 25 000	Total operating costs
	£ 11 000	Trading profit
	£ 1 000	Other income
	£ 12 000	Total income
Interest payable	£ 3 000	
	£ 9 000	Net profit before tax
Tax	£ 3 000	
Net profit	£ 6 000	

'Four profits!' Simon chuckled. 'No wonder poor old Marcus got so confused.'

'It could be more than four,' Jenny soberly told him. 'I've given a simplified P&L. There's net profit before interest and tax, and, if there had been extraordinary items, there would have been another profit – profit on extraordinary activities.'

'Well,' Simon spread his hands, 'where do we go from here?'

'Where we go from here is a projected P&L and an apprecia- tion of its importance,' Jenny replied. 'First of all, what's most important?'

'Increasing turnover,' Simon confidently replied. 'That way, you'll automatically increase your profits.'

'Are you sure?' Robin asked. 'Marcus was obsessed with increasing turnover. What did he call it – grabbing market share? But it didn't stop him being in continual trouble with the banks.'

'That's true,' Mary put in. 'Marcus took me to see the bank manager a couple of times on the basis that I would use some female charm on him. But it was hopeless. Because Marcus wouldn't show me – or anyone else – the accounts, I didn't know what I was talking about. The bank manager told us we were overtrading. I'm not sure what he meant but he certainly wasn't going to lend Marcus any more money. He told him to cut his costs instead.'

Jenny smiled wryly. 'Several valuable points there. Let's leave overtrading for the moment. We'll come back to it when we discuss cash flow later. Increasing turnover to grab market share may be justified as a strategic option – but it's usually only done through reducing prices or increasing marketing spend. Either way, the ratio of net profit to turnover is apt to be diminished. If,' she turned to Simon, 'we could increase turnover while keeping costs constant, or even in proportion, then yes, profits would be increased. But costs have a depressing tendency to increase at a faster rate than turnover. Cost control is an absolute must for any properly run business.'

She looked at Mary. 'Perhaps the worst aspect of secrecy is that people in the company can't make a connection between what they're doing and the financial costs and outcomes. This is incredibly dangerous. People will, in good faith, run up costs which cannot be sustained. I once worked for a company which was highly secretive about its finances. The result was that one department head recruited two very well paid high flyers in the same week that a mass redundancy was announced. You can imagine the effect that had on peoples' morale. As it happened, I was one of the high flyers. So, from here on, remember, it's tight financial control, which means equally tight operational control. People must know the financial position of the company, they must know how their area affects that financial position and they must be able to draw a clear connection between what they do and the financial results.'

Robin whistled. 'Marcus, stroll on!'

Reference
Reid, W. and Myddelton, D.R. (1992), *The Meaning Of Company Accounts*, 5th edition. Aldershot: Gower Publishing Ltd.

■ 13

The cashflow forecast

■ *How to manage cash*

Whereas the balance sheet describes the overall financial state of a concern and the P&L describes its profitability, the cashflow forecast describes its cash position. Does this matter? Well, yes it does matter, possibly even more than the balance sheet or the P&L. Why should this be so? Is cash not merely a feature of current assets and a fairly minor feature at that?

The truth is that cash is the very life blood of a business. A business may be extremely profitable yet, if it runs out of cash, it will not be able to meet its debts. When debts are not met, people get annoyed. Suppliers refuse to supply; employees vanish. Bank managers will show as much sympathy as sharks.

History is littered with examples of businesses, some formerly numbered among the great and the good, which foundered because of poor cash management. Profits tomorrow are no good when it is cash which is needed today.

Why is cash management so important? Because businesses rarely operate on a cash basis. There is an age of credit (how long we take to pay our suppliers) and an age of debt (how long our customers take to pay us). If the age of credit is longer than the age of debt, our cash management is healthy; we are getting paid faster than we are paying others. If all goes well, we can operate on negative working capital; in many businesses however, this is not possible.

The alternative position is when the age of debt is greater than the age of credit. Here our customers are taking much longer to pay us than we are taking to pay our suppliers. Dangerous. How will we meet our commitments in the meantime? If we take the time-honoured route of running the business from an overdraft, we have to pay for it and run the risk of having the proverbial plug pulled.

How to manage cash using the cash flow forecast

Having dealt with the P&L at the finance workshop (see 12 The profit and loss account), Jenny, Mary, Robin and Simon carried on to look at cash management, as shown in Table 13.1.

TABLE 13.1 THE CASHFLOW FORECAST

Period	1	2	3	4	5	6	7
Cash In	£10K	£0K	£0K	£10K	£12K	£12K	£14K
Cash Out	£5K	£7K	£9K	£9K	£9K	£10K	£10K
Net	£5K	£(2)K	£(11)K	£(10)K	£(7)K	£(5)K	£(1)K

'I just can't see the problem,' Simon insisted. 'According to the projection we've developed, Jenny, the business is perfectly sound. Our first month's sales amount to £10 000. The cost of sales is £7 000. Therefore we are making a good profit. The next month's sales are £12 000 and cost of sales are £9 000. So again we're making a good profit. And so it goes.'

Inwardly, Jenny sighed. There were always some who seemed to resist the harsh lesson. 'We have begun the period with an overdraft of £10 000. Our age of credit is a month, i.e. we are paying our suppliers in a month. Our age of debt is three months, i.e. it is taking three months for our customers to pay us – perfectly normal for many commercial organizations and most local authorities. Our profitability is fine; our cashflow forecast shows a deficit for the first seven months.'

'A shrinking deficit,' Simon put in. 'That I agree. A shrinking deficit,' Jenny assented. 'But a deficit nonetheless. And a deficit which must be made good if the business is to survive.'

'What you are saying is that either we have a further injection of working capital or we manage the cash better,' Mary suggested. Jenny turned to her.

'That's right. If you were working from an overdraft, you would need £2 000 more in month 2, rising to £11 000 more in month 3 and falling after that.'

'What about bumping up the sales a bit?' Simon suggested. 'It would just make things worse,' Robin cut in, with barely concealed sarcasm. 'You'd be cutting your throat faster.' 'OK, wise guy,' Simon retorted. 'Go for a bigger overdraft. If it was good enough for Marcus, it was good enough for us.'

'Fine,' Jenny replied. 'I'm your friendly bank manager. I give you an extra £11 000. In month 6 however, there's a change of policy or a new broom. No more top-up loans of over £4 000 to businesses like yours.'

'But we're almost at that level,' Simon protested. 'I don't care,' Jenny shot back and now there was steel in her voice. 'It's not my business. I've pulled the plug. I had to be seen to be doing something and I did.' The trio stared wide eyed at her. 'Would a bank do that?' 'They would, they have, they do and they will,' she confirmed.

'Other points. This is a cashflow forecast for a new business – notoriously risky. Sales will take longer – much longer than you expect. The set-up cost in month 1 might increase by a factor of three. Quality might be poor and you're stuck with a pile of customer returns. No money there. One of your customers might go out of business. No money there, either. You might have underestimated the money you need to live on – or have a greater financial need. You might be tempted into overtrading, widening the gap between paying and being paid.'

'You're telling us to watch the cash like a hawk?' Mary asked. 'Yes I am, ' Jenny soberly told her.

Reference
Reid, W. and Myddelton, D.R. (1992), *The Meaning Of Company Accounts*, 5th edition, Aldershot: Gower Publishing Ltd.

■ 14

Investment appraisal

■ How to manage investment

Capital investment is an inevitable part of business life. Formerly it was left to senior managers. Now, like much else, many capital investment decisions are being devolved to the level of management which will be responsible for the outcomes. If some new machinery is to be bought, it is far better for the people who will be using the machinery to be involved in the decision making process. They will have psychological ownership of the machinery. They will appreciate it.

Money will always be in scarce supply so there will always be competing investment requests. Investment appraisal considers the likely monetary outflows and inflows and makes decisions based upon likely levels of return and perceived risk. That is all that anyone can do. It is certainly far better to approach investment appraisal in an intellectually honest fashion than to let dubious investments get pushed through because of politicking; the latter is a well worn route to disaster.

How to manage investments through investment appraisal

Having dealt with the cashflow forecast at the finance workshop (see 13 The cashflow forecast), Jenny, Mary, Robin and Simon carried on to look at investment appraisal. Jenny showed them two examples of investment appraisal, involving investment A and investment B. These are shown in Table 14.1.
0

TABLE 14.1 INVESTMENT APPRAISAL

Investment A

Period	1	2	3	4	5	6
Outflow	£10K	£8K	£6K			
Inflow	£3K	£6K	£9K	£9K	£12K	£12K
Net return	£(7)K	£(9)K	£(6)K	£3K	£15K	£27K

Investment B

Period	1	2	3	4	5	6
Outflow	£6K	£6K	£6K	£6K		
Inflow	£3K	£4K	£5K	£10K	£10K	£7K
Net return	£(3)K	£(5)K	£(6)K	£(2)K	£8K	£15K

'I would go for investment A,' Simon confidently asserted. 'No question about that. You're getting £27K out as against £15K. That's a much better deal in my book.'

'You'd be tying your money up much longer,' Robin pointed out.' 'Doesn't matter, if it's worth it,' Simon retorted. 'Actually, I'm not sure about that,' Mary interpolated. 'With investment A, you're only putting money in for three periods; with investment B, it's four.' 'True. But with investment A, your initial investment is bigger,' Robin pointed out. 'Yes,' Mary thoughtfully replied. ' I see what you mean.'

'Investment appraisal isn't easy,' Jenny told them. 'There are several criteria and they usually conflict. One criterion is the return on investment. In this example, the total investment is the same in both cases – £24K. Investment A yields £27K net return while investment B yields £15K. So, on a pure return on investment basis, investment A is obviously better.' At this, Simon couldn't resist a smirk.

'Another facet is timing – particularly the timing of cash flows. Investment A requires much more cash initially but investment B goes on for a period longer. If we look at the net situation, with investment A, we are a maximum of £9K out of pocket while with investment B, we're a maximum of £6K out of pocket.'

'Investment A looks a high risk, high return option, compared with investment B,' Mary ventured.

'I agree,' Jenny assented. 'That's the way it looks to me too. Of course,' she continued, 'that's looking at the investments from the point of perceived financial risk. Investment B might hold a technological risk far greater than anything in investment A. And there might be other mitigating factors. Investment A might involve a machine from Milan while investment B might involve a machine from the local town. Then again, after sales service might be better from Milan while the local supplier might go out of business.'

'You're saying it's all about risk?' Robin queried. 'I'm saying it's all about risk and return,' Jenny replied. 'Risk and return must fit into your corporate strategy. Sometimes doing nothing involves the greatest risk.'

There are innumerable methods of investment appraisal. One of the simplest is the payback – how long is it before you get your money back. Another is NPV – the net present value of future money, i.e. what that money would be worth today if it were discounted for inflation. But however you approach investment appraisal, do not be guided by solely financial considerations. Invest in business for operational reasons. And never forget common sense.

Reference
Mott, G. (1987), *Investment Appraisal For Managers*, Aldershot: Gower Publishing Ltd.

■ 15

The budget process

■ *How to manage budgets*

The budget process looks at the activities of an enterprise, whether profit-making or not, in terms of what funds will be needed and what funds will result. It is, by its very nature, a planning process, typically performed yearly and reviewed monthly. It should be done in a holistic fashion, encompassing all the activities of the enterprise and it should be done both top-down and bottom-up. By its very nature it needs to be iterative. It should not be regarded as carved in stone; nor should it be ignored or significantly changed on a whim or a passing need. The more experienced people are at budgeting, the more rigorous yet the more flexible will they tend to be. A budget is a necessary means to a chosen end. It is not an end in its own right.

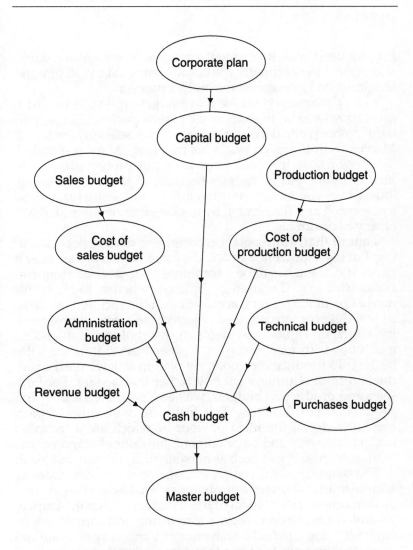

FIGURE 15.1 THE BUDGET PROCESS

How to manage budgets through the budget process

Having dealt with investment appraisal at the finance workshop (see 14 Investment appraisal), Jenny, Mary, Robin and Simon started to examine the budget process.

'I can't remember old Marcus budgeting – or if he did it must have been on the back of a cigarette packet,' Simon mordantly observed. 'I've got to say I can see why, now.' 'If Marcus didn't budget, that's his problem,' Mary responded. 'Sooner or later it would have been our problem too when luck ran out.' 'All businesses need luck,' Jenny pointed out, 'but it's unwise to rely on it too much. Budgeting makes you forewarned and forearmed. In an ever-changing world, that's all any of us can be.'

'I admit that, at first glance, budgeting does appear daunting. But it's logical enough and the more you do it, the easier it gets. First, there has to be a corporate plan, devised from corporate strategy. The strategic options (whether to be in this market or that, mergers, acquisitions, refinancing, you name it) will devolve into planned objectives in terms of profitability, return on capital, payments to shareholders and lending institutions. To meet the plan, we need sales; thus the sales budget. To produce the goods we plan to sell, we need a production budget (unless we buy rather than make). For both sales and production budgets, we need associated selling and production cost budgets. This leaves us with other departmental budgets, the most obvious of which are a technical budget (research and development, for example) and central management services such as personnel, IT, finance and legal.

'I have grouped the central management services under an administration budget but obviously that would be further broken down, as would all of these budgets. After the emphasis which I made on cashflow forecasting and control, it's no surprise, I hope, to find a cash budget. Obviously revenue and purchases budgets feed into that. Finally there's a master budget which summarizes all of the other budgets and will, in turn, devolve into a balance sheet, a P&L and a source and application of funds statement (where the money comes from and where it goes to).'

'So the proof of a well done budgeting process is presumably how well the master budget underwrites the corporate plan?' asked Mary.

'Absolutely,' Jenny replied. 'But budgets must reflect commercial reality. It is no use postulating hockey stick sales curves and banking on recoveries which always seem to be expected in the third quarter?'

'What, in heaven's name, is a hockey stick sales curve?' Simon lazily asked. 'A sales plan which starts with modest sales, which then take off dramatically, thus producing a shape like a hockey stick,' Mary tersely told him, leaving him little the wiser.

'Responsibility is the key,' Jenny asserted. 'Responsibility and prudence. Aim for the possible, not the impossible. And then track the funds against the budgeted amounts. You'll learn a lot, that way, I assure you. Just wait and see!'

Reference
Sizer, J. (1969), *An Insight Into Management Accounting*, London: Penguin Books.

PART V

Managing operations

■ 16

The closed system

■ *How to add value*

Whereas the open system (see 1 The open system) looks at an organization in terms of its relationships with the outside world, the closed system views an organization in terms of its internal operations. Do not be deceived by the apparent obviousness and simplicity of open and closed systems. Taken individually or preferably together, they constitute two extraordinarily powerful management models.

The closed system regards all organizations as having inputs, processes and outputs. The classic inputs are people, materials, machines and money. These will apply to virtually all organizations, whether public or private, profit-making or not. Printed circuit boards and numerically controlled machines may be the principal materials and machines in a private sector, profit-making electronics plant. Paper and wordprocessors may be the principal materials and machines in a public sector, non-profit making think tank. Both will have both people and money as inputs. People and money appear to be inescapable inputs for any organization.

INPUT	PROCESS	OUTPUT
People	Added Value	Finished goods
Materials		Sales
Machines		Turnover
		Profit

Money – – – – – – – – – – – – – – – – – More money

FIGURE 16.1 THE CLOSED SYSTEM

When it comes to processes however, organizations differ widely. Raw materials, for instance circuit boards, are worked upon. They may go through several stages of operations as work in progress before they end up as finished stock. Along the way, they have accumulated **added value**. A unit is worth more as work in progress than it was as raw material. It is worth still more as finished stock than it was worth as work in progress. Of course such added value can only be realized when the units are sold, but the principle of added value makes sense. Manufacturing is not just about making things; in a far greater sense, it is about adding value.

With a non-profit making organization, the concept of **added social value** is probably more useful. Clearly neither the police force nor a drug rehabilitation unit should exist to make a profit. But a drug rehabilitation unit which helps drug abusers to reform themselves and lead more productive and fulfilling lives is taking inputs (users) and adding value of a different kind. Obviously in society we need to find a balance between organizations which add value and those which add social value. What that balance should be is a political question which we must individually and collectively answer.

Added social value can be much harder to define than added value. That should not deter us from making the effort.

Conventional private sector, profit-making organizations' outputs are as shown in Figure 16.1. Finished goods, sales, turnover and profit ultimately translate into money which we have realized from the enterprise. Money out can be related to money in as, for example, gross and net profitability and return on capital. Relating outputs to inputs will give us control over the process. The more senior the manager, the greater the timespan of control, for instance return on capital/a year for a managing director versus units per operative per hour/shift for a supervisor.

With an organization which produces added social value, it is no less important that outputs are measured. In fact, the golden rule must always be: if resources are utilized as inputs, then outputs must be measured. The closed system, which gives us a strictly local, operational view of an organization, also gives us a beautifully simple model to use when considering resource utilization. Management, by its very nature, has always and will always have to regard resource usage as a fundamental concern.

How to add value using the closed system

Manton Radiators was a well known company which had fallen upon hard times. It had always been a family concern; Simon Manton, the chairman, was third generation. He intended to leave the company to Herbert Manton, his son, that is if there was anything to leave, he gloomily reflected.

As is often the case, consultants were called in, somewhat on the late side, as, unfortunately, is also often the case. Their analysis of Manton was particularly bitter to Simon. But, he wryly reflected, it was also fair.

In particular, the consultants focused upon manufacturing

practices. Poor plant layout, obsolete working practices, skill demarcation and an approach to training which owed more to assimilating Nellie's faults than her supposed virtues.

In retraining the workforce, substantial use was made of the concept of adding value via use of the closed system. In particular, much work had to be done with the supervisors. Hitherto they had regarded themselves as machine setters and progress chasers, expediting radiators. These roles were now redundant. What was far more important was for supervisors to control the process of added value and thereby obtain the best ratio of outputs to inputs. To do that, they obviously had to know their inputs and outputs, both operationally and financially. This involved disseminating what had formerly been regarded as top secret information.

'We never intended it to be top secret,' Simon Manton demurred, 'we just thought they didn't need to know. However, I now accept that they do need to know.'

Retraining the supervisors proved to be a long and arduous enterprise. It was hardly their fault that they were doing jobs which were at best irrelevant and at worst counterproductive. Much work also needed to be done with other departments and levels of management besides involving the workforce, who were, after all, the only people directly adding value. But, as the controllers of production in a manufacturing company, the supervisors occupied the key management position. Changing their behaviour from making radiators to making money through making radiators was no easy task. The proof of the pudding is ever in the eating. When Manton made radiators, they were firmly on the road to doom. When they decided to make money through making radiators, they zoomed into profit. Adding value through the closed system was a pivotal management instrument in enabling them to do so.

'Adding value is paramount,' Simon Manton admitted, exactly a year after the consultants arrived on site. 'You people have convinced me of that. And the results say likewise. Perhaps it's taken us a long time to see what we should have seen in the first place. Still, better late than never!'

Reference
Walley, B. (1986), *Production Management Handbook*, Aldershot:
    Gower Publishing Ltd.

■ 17

The management control cycle

■ *How to add value*

All operations have inputs, processes and outputs. Unless processes are tightly controlled in terms of outputs against inputs, one of two situations occurs. Either inadequate outputs are achieved with the given input resources, or outputs are achieved with an unacceptably high level of input resource. Any organization which does not have management control systems relating outputs to inputs will have a much higher level of resource usage than it needs.

Many people confuse management control systems (MCS) with management information systems (MIS). MIS tell us many interesting things about the process. MCS give us vital information about the success of the process in terms of timeliness and resource usage.

The management control cycle provides a skeleton around which a management control system can be constructed. Its elements are as follows.

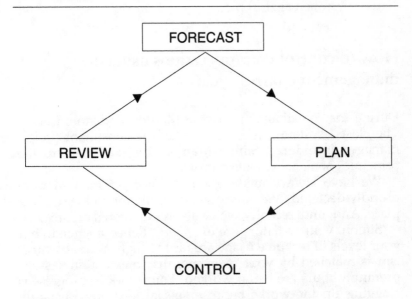

FIGURE 17.1 THE MANAGEMENT CONTROL CYCLE

Forecast is our best estimate of what we think will happen. Usually it relates to market demand. If we have a sales forecast that our customers will demand 30 per cent extra product over the next six months, then obviously we need to be thinking about how we are going to manufacture such product.

Plan is what we intend to do. It is a statement of intent. It is not what we think might happen (forecast). It is what we are going to make happen, for instance manufacture.

Control is the constant monitoring of plan against actual, followed by immediate remedial action to negate variance. Usually the plan is broken down into relatively small and manageable segments with short timeframes.

Review looks at two relationships. How accurate was the original forecast, against what transpired? And how well was actual controlled against plan?

How to control your operations using the management control cycle

During the consultancy project at Manton Radiators (see 16 The closed system), Rebecca Hawke, the consultant project manager, introduced Simon Manton, the chairman, to the principles of management control.

'We have always made good radiators,' Simon Manton proudly declared. 'We have a good reputation in the marketplace. And, until recently, we've always delivered on time.'

'Simon, your radiators are excellent,' Rebecca agreed, 'but your levels of resource usage are far too high. Your absenteeism is matched by your overtime; that means unnecessary premium hours are being worked. Your work in progress is clogging up the works because special jobs are constantly being pushed through. And your finished stock is a buffer.' She paused significantly. 'A very expensive buffer at that. Working capital is enormous. You should be working on negative working capital.' 'Negative working capital?' Simon blanched as though Rebecca was introducing him to a Martian.

Through a series of lengthy and, at times, painful discussions, Rebecca convinced Simon that production planning and control were imprecise at best, *ad hoc* at worst. Installing a management control system based upon the forecast, plan, control, review cycle proved equally traumatic for the supervisors and managers, although, by and large, it was welcomed by the workforce. 'At least now we know what the hell's going on,' growled Silas Rhodes.

Rebecca found that much of her time had to be spent emphasizing the difference between forecasting and planning. 'It's a forecast until we write our names on it in blood,' she insisted, only half joking, 'then it's a plan.' Similarly, she had to disabuse people of the fallacy that planning merely involved the production of plans. 'It is no use producing plans and then going off to do something else because reality is different. Forecasting and planning should be like the lenses in a high powered telescope – constantly adjusted, to keep reality in focus.'

Similarly, she had to emphasize the difference between control and review. 'Review is what you used to do – all those boring monthly meetings with detailed statistics about what went wrong and absolute powerlessness to do anything about it. Control is what happens, minute by minute, out there on the shop floor – the only place where value is being added. It certainly isn't being added here,' she tactlessly noted to the discomfited members of the Manton boardroom.

In time, control systems were developed with supervisors and workforce. In time, control went right onto the shop floor – the place where it truly belongs.

Reference
Walley, B. (1986), *Production Management Handbook*, Aldershot: Gower Publishing Ltd.

■ 18

Operational meetings

■ *How to control your operations*

The temptation with managing operations is to let them manage you. Few, if any, operational managers are immune from this temptation. With day to day demands, people become so lost in the process (see 16 The closed system), that they lose sight of the output/input balance. Then they start to throw money at problems. Often such money is called overtime.

Another sign that the war is being lost is poor time management where there is never time for even one of poor old Ivy Lee's six tasks (see 40 The Ivy Lee method) and there is no such thing as importance, only urgency (see 41 The priority grid). Strangely enough, however, there is all the time in the world to carp at what has gone wrong and rework it.

The management control cycle provides a mechanism to manage operations – any operation. Output/input measures provide control indices. For a supervisor, these might be units per paid hour, per shift. For a production director, it might be contribution against budget.

All that a management control system can do is provide a

structured mechanism for resolving problems. The forum for resolving such problems is undoubtedly meetings. Often operational meetings are *ad hoc* and ill informed. Usually they are post mortems about what went wrong, when it's too late to put it right. Rarely are operational meetings properly integrated.

TABLE 18.1 OPERATIONAL MEETINGS

Span of control	Who present	How often
All production areas	Production director/ managers	Weekly
Each production area	Production manager, supervisors, planner	Daily
Each work area.	Supervisor, workforce	Shift

The (simplified) operational meeting model shown in Table 18.1 is properly integrated. It runs from shop floor to production director. It runs from shift (with hourly information) to day to week. It enables each person in the chain of command to focus upon his or her role, with relevant information and a relevant time span. Best of all, it works! It does, however, invariably need a considerable commitment to developing meeting skills (see 30 Meeting skills).

How to control your operations using operational meetings

During the consultancy project at Manton Radiators (see 16 The closed system), Rebecca Hawke, the consultant project manager, introduced the subject of management meetings to the Manton family, owners and managers of Manton Radiators.

'You can't tell us about meetings,' Simon Manton smugly retorted. 'We know all about meetings. In fact, a couple of years ago we had someone, just like you, in to teach us how to run briefings.' 'Briefings,' Rebecca snorted with derision. 'Briefings,' Simon returned, a little taken aback. (In their encounters to date, he always seemed to have come off worst. Perhaps the unhappy trend wasn't going to be reversed after all.)

'Why have a meeting?' Rebecca asked. 'What meeting?' 'Any meeting. Any meeting at all.' 'Well, to keep people informed – to find out what's going on. To issue directives.' Simon eyed her narrowly. 'Why don't you tell me why have a meeting?'

'I think there are only two reasons to have a meeting.' Rebecca flicked a spot of dust from the boardroom table. 'One reason is to communicate and communicate only, put people in the picture as it were.' Simon nodded sagely. 'Such a meeting I would call a briefing meeting.' Again Simon nodded.

'The other kind of meeting,' Rebecca continued remorselessly, 'I would call an operational meeting. Here the purpose of the meeting is to make decisions. Obviously, in order to make decisions, one must communicate. But the crucial difference between the two types of meetings is this: with briefing meetings, we don't want decisions, with operational meetings we do.'

'The problem here is that your meetings fall between these two types. Your monthly management meetings are postmortems, your briefing meetings are state of the nation efforts, constantly interrupted by trivial local problems.' 'How do you know what our briefing meetings are like?' Simon asked. 'I've been to three so far,' Rebecca retorted.

Rebecca started with daily operational meetings in one production area. The manager, the planner and the morning shift supervisor reviewed the previous 24 hours and produced a plan for the following 24 hours. The wide initial variance between plan and actual produced a flood of actions, many of them relating to the maintenance department. 'One golden rule though,' Rebecca insisted. 'We can't allocate actions to people who aren't at the meeting.' 'So surely we should have an engineer at our morning meeting?' Jim Walpole, the production manager queried. 'You tell me, Jim,' Rebecca enigmatically replied. 'Is it a production meeting or an engineering meeting?'

Rebecca swifly moved from daily production meetings to shift meetings with supervisors and work teams. The shift management control information generated, together with concomitant problem resolution, greatly aided the production meeting. This was proved when the average daily number of actions fell from 17 to five.

Once she had daily and shift meetings working in one production area, Rebecca extended them to the other areas, making use of her initial trainees as role models and, in some cases, trainers. When she had developed good shift and daily meetings in all of the production areas, she developed the weekly meetings between the production director and his managers. Then, having assembled all the pieces of the jigsaw, she made sure the fit was tight.

'You must be pleased with yourself,' Simon remarked, some months of hard work later. 'The benefits in productivity are quite astounding. Now that you've done production, what next?' 'Simon, I haven't remotely come near to having finished with production,' Rebecca retorted. 'Two other thoughts for you. Operational meetings – and management control systems – apply to any operations, not just production areas. And where should the meetings structure end – and start, for that matter?'

'The boardroom, I suppose,' Simon mechanically agreed. 'So then we would have an unbroken, dynamic mechanism from boardroom to shop floor, wouldn't we?' Rebecca replied. 'Hmm.' Simon mused. 'I must say, I never thought of it quite like that before.'

Reference
Johns, D.T. and Harding, H.A. (1989), *Operations Management*, Aldershot: Gower Publishing Ltd.

■ 19

Action teams

■ *How to solve problems/make improvements*

Most organizations have long running problems which seemingly cannot be properly eradicated. The planned maintenance system which doesn't work; the poor liasion between design and production or between technical and marketing which will cause tangible operational problems that recur month in and month out, year in and year out. Occasionally, goaded by a particularly savage interdepartmental memo, or the arrival of a senior manager, there will be a purge. But such purges tend to be short lived indeed. Usually little progress is made and soon everything reverts to normal.

The problem with these problems is twofold. Firstly, they cause an inordinate amount of wasted effort (and money). Secondly, they cause individual burnout of the 'why bother hitting your head against a brick wall' variety. Collectively these two aspects result in organizational blockage – a severe constraint to development and progress.

Action teams provide a means of overcoming this malaise. An operational problem is raised in a dedicated meeting by the group which is experiencing it. They define their problem as best they can – both qualitatively and quantitatively. They list all the other groups which they believe either affect or are affected by this problem – the stakeholder groups. They then nominate a representative. This representative calls a further meeting with other individuals whom s/he feels are representatives of all of the other stakeholder groups. S/he outlines the problem as perceived by the group which has raised it and asks the other representatives to help redefine and solve the problem for everybody's benefit and, not least, the organization's.

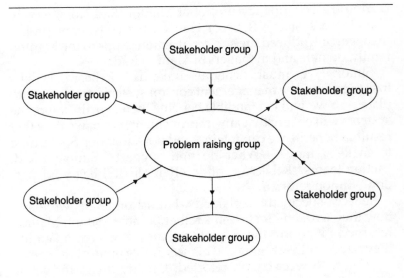

FIGURE 19.1 ACTION TEAMS

The idea is for the representatives to form an action team – to address a particular problem. The life of the action team is the life of the problem. When the action team has investigated the problem and come up with a proposed solution, the easy part has been done. The hard part is implementation. Each representative has to go back to his or her stakeholder group, explain the solution and enlist the aid of the group members in implementing it. Only when action team members can report to the team that the solution has been successfully implemented by the stakeholder groups can the action team disband with a problem solved/opportunity gained – and a resultant benefit.

How to solve problems/make improvements by using action teams

During the consultancy project at Manton Radiators, (see 16 The closed system), Rebecca Hawke, the consultant project manager, introduced the subject of action teams to the Manton family, owners and managers of Manton Radiators.

'Simon, we must generate impetus,' Rebecca Hawke insisted. 'Fine, the management control systems are going into place – so we will get tangible benefits there. Furthermore the systems will ensure that any improvements we make now will result in benefits we can retain – and not squander. So it's time to make a move.' 'What do you suggest?' Simon asked. 'Action teams,' Rebecca confidently replied. 'I beg your pardon?' Simon retorted.

Rebecca succinctly explained what action teams were and how they worked. 'It all seems rather familiar,' Simon Manton returned. 'We introduced quality circles some years ago but they never really caught on. This seems like more of the same.'

'It isn't,' Rebecca crisply retorted. 'Quality circles and action teams are fundamentally different. Quality circles are people looking for problems; action teams are problems looking for people. Quality circles ultimately fail because of the glass walls between different departments and groups; action teams encompass members from all relevant areas. Quality circles ramble on until they run out of steam; action teams are focused and problem-specific. When the problem has been solved, they disband. And so – on to the next problem!'

Simon sighed. 'As ever, Rebecca, you make me feel that what little I know isn't really worth knowing.' 'Come on, Simon,' Rebecca chided. ' Weltschmerz before nine o' clock in the morning isn't becoming. Besides,' she glanced pointedly at her watch. ' We do have work to do.'

Knowing that the company had flirted with quality circles and failed, Rebecca set her stall out carefully. No, she wasn't against Japanese management methods, she was merely for sound management methods, irrespective of their pedigree. She wasn't against quality circles *per se*, she simply felt that cultural problems often curtailed their usefulness and, in any case, action teams were almost always more effective. But, as she stressed, theory was theory and practice was practice.

Aware that the first action team would have to be carefully chosen and nurtured, she thought long and hard. Action team members needed to be effective representatives of their stakeholder groups. They also had to work well within the action team itself. So, besides their relevant functional expertise, they would need to be team players within the action team and influencers within the stakeholder groups. They would certainly need to communicate well and sell benefits to the 'back home' people, so they would need sales training (see 8 Features and benefits). They would also need teambuilding sessions (see 31 Team formation).

In truth, the first action team was a success for one reason and one reason only. Rebecca, in her desire that it should be a success, nurtured it with lavish care, skill and attention. But when the benefits generated by the first action team were publicized within the organization, people really began to sit up and take notice. The next action team went more smoothly and the following one more smoothly still. 'Hurrah,' Rebecca silently toasted herself with a beaker of coffee in the supervisors' cabin. And then she remembered. 'It's not my success which matters; it's theirs.'

Reference
Robson, M. (1993), *Problem Solving In Groups*, Aldershot: Gower Publishing Ltd.

■ 20

The Gantt chart

■ *How to project manage*

The Gantt chart, named after Henry Gantt, a pioneer of work study, is simplicity itself. Projects (an advertising campaign, a site relocation, a takeover bid) are split into their constituent elements. The elements are then timetabled.

Simple, yes. But there is rather more to project management than merely devising a neat chart. Major construction projects (the sort which regularly feature in the national press) invariably seem to overrun by at least 30 per cent on time and 50 per cent on cost. If major construction contractors, whose very business is project management, can't seem to get it right, is there any hope for the rest of us?

There has to be and there is. There has to be, because operational management can be divided into the management of routine, day to day operations and the management of discrete projects. Management control systems and an attendent meetings infrastructure will enable us to manage the day to day. Project management will enable us to control those unsettling one-offs.

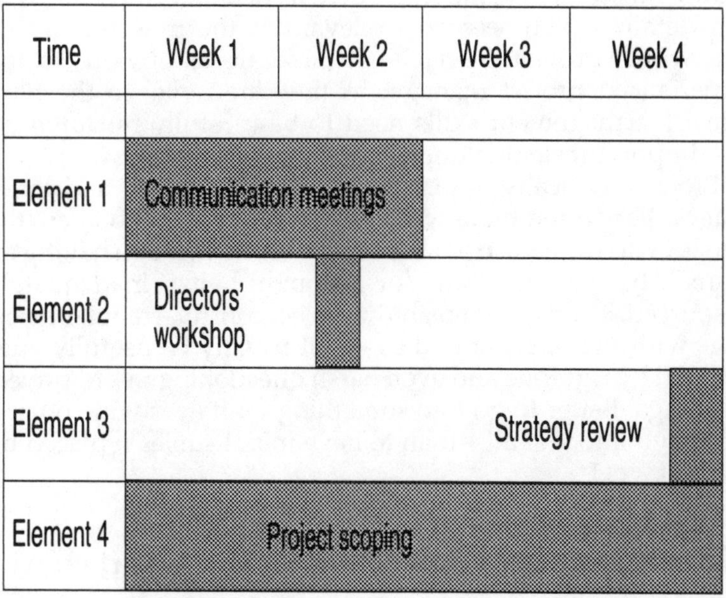

Time	Week 1	Week 2	Week 3	Week 4
Element 1	Communication meetings			
Element 2	Directors' workshop			
Element 3			Strategy review	
Element 4	Project scoping			

FIGURE 20.1 THE GANTT CHART

Any project must have an objective. That objective must be measureable, time-based and attributable. To be measurable, a project must be either quantitative (sell 6000 hardback copies), or it should be success/fail (we won/didn't win). To be time-based, the elements must be capable of being logged on to a Gantt chart. To be attributable, someone must be, as project manager, solely accountable for the delivery of results. Project management by committee is a charter for inaction.

Although the project manager is accountable for ultimate delivery, other people (for instance, subcontractors) may be accountable for delivery of elements. Should a project be imperilled because of tardy delivery of elements, it is no use the project manager wailing. S/he is still accountable!

If people are unused to managing projects, it is likely that their first attempts will be disasters. The empty promises, the bland 'no problems', the shifty denials of blame, those intriguing details which seemed irrelevant at the time but which afterwards proved crucial – all these are as obvious to the experienced project manager as they are novel to the tyro. Project management skills need to be carefully nurtured on less important elements and initially small projects.

Projects typically appear to fail in the middle and latter stages. Very often there will have been people who knew the project was dubious from the onset – either through having an unrealistic objective and/or through being inadequately resourced. The typical means of project control – regular meetings with the relevant bodies – will usually be usefully augmented by rigorous and even harsh questioning in pre-project meetings. Better to go into something with eyes wide open – or not go into it at all – than to have initial smiles replaced by tears of woe!

How to manage projects using the Gantt chart

During the consultancy project at Manton Radiators (see 16 The closed system), Rebecca Hawke, the consultant project manager, introduced the subject of project management to the Manton family, owners and managers of Manton Radiators.

'Fifty-nine engineering projects! Fifty-nine, for heaven's sake. Why not a hundred and fifty-nine? Or, better still, a thousand and fifty-nine?' 'Don't be like that, Rebecca,' Hubert Manton protested. 'Aye, Rebecca, don't get downhearted,' Bertie Manton chipped in.

Rebecca looked at them wonderingly. 'Do you know the average life of an engineering project around here?' Hubert shrugged. 'Oh, a couple of months, I suppose. A few months,' he amended. Bertie nodded sagely.

'Well, I have news for you gentlemen,' Rebecca replied. 'Out of the last 13 projects deemed to be completed not one was achieved in less than six months. Indeed, in about six of them, there seems to be considerable doubt that they are actually completed.'

'At six months a project, that makes some 30 years. Thirty years of projects,' she mused. 'A few customers will be kept waiting.' 'They are internal customers,' Hubert carefully pointed out. 'Internal customers!' Rebecca snorted. 'That makes it even worse. If we can't deliver with our internal customers, what chance do we have with our external customers?'

'Let's look at it this way,' she continued. 'We have a certain number of engineers. Therefore, give or take a little, we have a certain number of engineering hours available. Those hours may be too few or too many. At present, I don't know. But,' she added bleakly, 'I have my suspicions. Well we certainly haven't got 30 years' worth of engineering hours to play with. Therefore I suggest we re-evaluate these projects.'

The re-evaluation process, which initially threatened to be complex and protracted, was abruptly curtailed by Rebecca pointing out that, in the current state of Manton Radiators, any project which could not yield a benefit within the financial year should be postponed. She then cost-benefitted the projects in terms of engineering hours and attendant costs against proposed benefits. Many more dropped by the wayside. Most painful of all for Bertie, the engineering director, were some of his pet projects which were deemed unviable.

'Deemed unviable by whom, I might ask?' he loftily enquired. 'Deemed unviable by your own project engineers,' Rebecca brutally told him.

They were finally left with eight projects. 'That means eight project managers and eight sets of weekly project control meetings,' Rebecca declared. 'Eight sets of weekly project meetings,' Bertie exclaimed. 'We don't have time for all that.' 'If you haven't time for all that, then you haven't time for the projects in the first place,' Rebecca told him.

Over the next few months, progress was slowly and painfully gained. Rebecca only felt that she was beginning to win when she heard one of the process engineers remark to a draftsman, 'It makes a change to finish something in time. I never thought I'd be looking forward to the next project!'

Reference

Lock, D. (1992), *Project Management*, 5th edition, Aldershot: Gower Publishing Ltd.

■ 21

Break-even analysis

■ *How to increase your profitability*

Break-even analysis is a simple and effective way of highlighting the profitability (or otherwise) of operations. It divides costs into fixed costs and variable costs. Fixed costs are costs which occur irrespective of output. Typical fixed costs would be rent, rates, and leasing charges relating to premises, plant and machinery. These costs relate to bills which have to be paid, regardless. Variable costs are costs which are directly related to output. An obvious variable cost in manufacturing industry is raw material. If we make 1 000 units, we will use 1 000 times more raw material than if we made one unit (assuming no economies of scale or scrap).

The division of costs into fixed and variable allows us to construct what is known as a break-even chart. In the break-even chart shown in Figure 21.1, a certain level of fixed cost is incurred, irrespective of output. This fixed cost line is shown as D—C. The variable cost line A—F, by contrast, is directly proportional to output. The total cost line, D—H, is created by adding the fixed cost line to the variable cost line. (Obviously, total cost = fixed cost + variable cost).

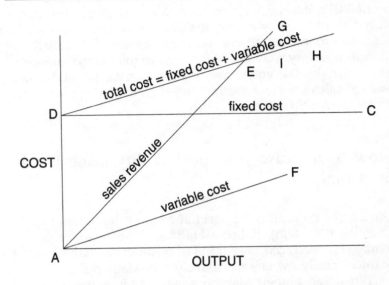

FIGURE 21.1 BREAK-EVEN ANALYSIS

The line A—E—G shows sales revenue as being directly proportional to output, which it will be if we sell each unit we make and keep the price constant. At point E, the sales revenue line cuts the total cost line. Thus, at E, sales revenue = total costs. We break even. We make neither a profit nor a loss. Obviously the aim of business is to make a profit, thereby achieving rather more than merely breaking even. Beyond E, this will be the case, as sales revenue will exceed total costs. Before E, total costs will exceed sales revenue and we will make a loss.

Two other points need to be noted about a break-even chart. The angle GEH is known as the **angle of incidence**. The greater this is, the greater the rate of profitability for each additional unit above break-even. Of course, this cuts both ways. The greater the angle of incidence, the greater will be the rate of loss if break-even is not reached!

The other noteworthy item in a break-even chart is what is called the **margin of safety**. If I represents our normal level of profitability, it is much closer to break-even either in units produced and sold or in money than H. The difference, either in units or money, between I and break-even at E is called the margin of safety. Obviously, the greater the margin of safety, the less risky the enterprise. If costs can be pushed down and/or sales revenues pushed up, then the margin of safety will improve. So will profitability!

How to increase your profitability using break-even analysis

During the consultancy project at Manton Radiators (see 16 The closed system), Rebecca Hawke, the consultant project manager, introduced the subject of break-even analysis to the Manton family, owners and managers of Manton Radiators.

'But why?' Hubert Manton asked. 'Why on earth do you want to run a session on break-even analysis with the supervisors?'

'Because I want to run sessions on break-even analysis with the operatives,' Rebecca undauntedly replied. 'And it's surely only right to see the supervisors first.'

'The operatives?' Hubert incredulously queried. 'You must be crazy!' Rebecca was ill disposed to argue the point. Instead she just went ahead.

The first session went surprisingly well. (Not that it really mattered, Rebecca reflected. If it hadn't, she would simply have had another session – and another, if need be.)

The break-even chart was relatively easily constructed and the questions were thoughtful and well informed. 'What about labour costs?' Sam Fulton, the C team supervisor, questioned. 'Are they fixed costs or variable costs?' 'Well, Sam,' Rebecca replied. 'How easy are they to switch on and off?' 'Not that easy,' he grunted. 'Well, we can lay an extra shift on, at a pinch. And we can ask people to work overtime. But that's about all.'

'Exactly,' Rebecca replied. 'They're variable, to some

degree, but mostly they're fixed. I think you will find the same with most fixed costs,' she suggested. 'We can usually affect them to some degree, but not much. For instance, we can negotiate better rates for power costs which will decrease our power bills for direct areas and indirect areas, like the offices. But that won't affect our overheads very much in the offices. We're pretty well stuck with them – unless,' she added thoughtfully, 'we can discover a radically different way of conducting our business.'

'Break-even analysis isn't exact,' she stressed. 'It makes assumptions, for instance, that there are no economies of scale and that the effects of mix remain constant. But, limitations aside, it's useful. Very useful.'

Let's take the situation considered. At fixed costs of £8 000, variable costs of £2.00 per unit and a sales price of £10.00 per unit, we have a break-even at 1 000 units or £10 000. We can show this as follows (see Table 21.1):

TABLE 21.1 BREAK-EVEN ANALYSIS – THE FIGURES

Units	Fixed Cost	Variable Cost	Total Cost	Sales Revenue	Profit
1 000	£8 000	£2 000	£10 000	£10 000	£0 00
1 100	£8 000	£2 200	£10 200	£11 000	£800
1 210	£8 000	£2 420	£10 420	£12 100	£1 680
990	£8 000	£1 980	£ 9 980	£ 9 900	£(80)

'At 1 000 units, we break even, so we neither make nor lose money,' she stressed. 'Now, let's assume that our normal production is 1 100 units per shift. As you can see, the margin of safety is quite low – it's 100 units, less than 10 per cent. Another way of putting it is that our break-even is about 90 per cent. Dangerous territory.'

'Let's see what happens when we increase production and sales by 10 per cent. We now make a profit of £1 680 as against our normal profit of £800. In other words, by increasing our output by 10 per cent, we increase our profitability by more than 100 per cent!'

Rebecca looked triumphantly around her. People were silent, rapt, aghast. She smiled. 'I bet you thought that you had to double production to double profit,' she suggested, with a wicked gleam in her eye. 'Aye, you're right there, lass,' one old diehard agreed. 'Not so,' Rebecca assured him. 'Not so.'

'Of course, it works the other way too. If we drop 10 per cent, we decimate our profit. In fact, we make a loss – of £80.' There was a low whistle of appreciation. Rebecca surveyed the room.

'As it happens, this is an almost exact model of the situation at Manton Radiators.' She casually flicked a switch, the projector showed a faithful mirror of her first break-even chart, but with realistic figures on it. 'So you're saying that if we increased production by 10 per cent we could double our profitability?' Rebecca nodded. 'Well, scrap is 6 per cent and rework is 15 per cent. Even if we saved half of those, there's about 10 per cent for the asking.' 'Now you're talking,' Rebecca agreed, 'and that's just a beginning!'

Meanwhile, up in the boardroom, Hubert was vociferously moaning to Charles and Hubert. 'Break-even charts with the supervisors and the shop floor! Whatever next!'

Reference
Walley, B. (1986), *Production Management Handbook*, Aldershot: Gower Publishing Ltd.

PART VI

Managing decisions

■ 22

The decision tree

■ *How to solve problems and make decisions*

A decision tree is a device for charting the various factors which go towards solving a problem and making a consequent decision. For many people, the hardest behavioural part is actually making a decision. The hardest cognitive part, however, is defining the problem. Problem solving and decision making are often treated as separate subjects in management writing. This seems strange. If a problem is solved, a decision will have to be made, even if it is merely to implement the solution. Often a choice must be made between competing solutions, which will have various pros and cons. Managers are paid to solve problems, make decisions and implement them. Usually the more senior the manager, the more harrowing the problems, decisions and implementations, either because the ambiguity is great ('should we locate the new plant in Iberia or Korea?') or, simply, because it is painful ('should we close the Blackburn site?').

If problems have been correctly defined, decisions are almost pitifully stark. They fall into either/or categories –

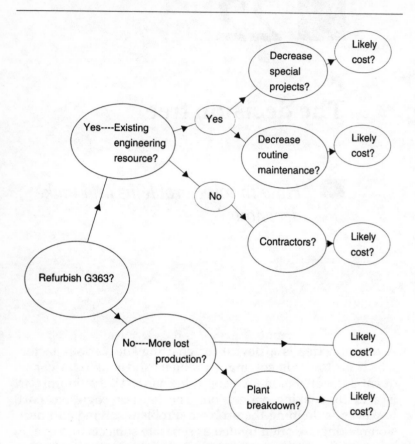

FIGURE 22.1 A DECISION TREE

either we do this or we don't or either we do this or we do that. Effective senior managers can assimilate complex issues and rapidly reduce them to either/or categories. Very often, they are implicitly using a decision tree. Practice has made them adroit at selecting the important elements and discarding the irrelevant.

Given that such people can make decision trees in their minds, it is no bad thing to draw them on paper. It doesn't take much longer and it is a good discipline. At the very least, it makes it far less likely that we will forget an important element.

How to solve problems and make decisions using the decision tree

Emile Ratón, the world famous professor of methodology, was conducting a workshop with the directors of an engineering company. Inevitably, the subject of projects cropped up.

'Projects. Always you talk about projects. This project and that project. This project as against that project. What to do and what not to do. If we are not careful we will be talking about projects until we are old men. The trick is not to talk about projects. The trick is to complete those which are truly worthwhile.'

Ratón stopped. To the assembled audience it seemed as though there was no air left in his lungs. They gazed in wonderment at the little professor. 'I really don't think it's as simple as all that,' Henry Hardacre, the technical director, rather nervously ventured.

'Then we must make it as simple as that,' Ratón told him with complete assurance. 'That is what management is about – making the complex simple. Normally, people make the simple complex; usually, the more intelligent they are, the more complex they make the simple. My friends,' he turned and spread his hands expansively. 'We must learn to do the opposite.'

'Let us take one project – the refurbishment of G363. We have a simple decision – either we refurbish it or we do not. If we refurbish it, then we could use existing engineering resource – resource which we might profitably expend elsewhere.'

'On the other hand, we can choose not to refurbish G363. If we make the choice, then we must accept the current levels of lost production and the accompanying dent in the levels of profitability. We also take the risk of plant breakdown for G363. This is a risk which carries a considerable penalty.

'Now, before our eyes, Michèle, my assistant, will draw a decision tree for the G363 project. And, please remember, this is one project among many. But we must start somewhere,' he gloomily concluded.

As bidden, Michèle drew up the decision tree for the G363 project. For the first time, the audience saw a structured way of approaching problems, a way which started with the decision and extrapolated to include all of the relevant variables.

'Structure,' Ratón stressed. 'We must approach problems in a structured fashion. We are professional problem solvers, not bar stool philosophers. We must abandon the cosy world of opinion and enter a world of known variables. Only then shall we prevail.'

Reference
Magee, J.F. (1964), *Decision Trees for Decision Making*, Harvard Business Review.

■ 23

The balance sheet method

■ *How to make the best decision*

When problems have been well defined and thoroughly investigated, decision making is simple – which is not to say that it cannot be very difficult. If there is only one possible decision, then it is an either/or – either we take it or we don't. If there are competing alternatives (there usually are), then it is either we take this decision, or that one, or the other one.

Any decision will have pros and cons. The balance sheet method is simplicity itself. Divide a piece of paper, or a whiteboard or flipchart, into two halves. One half is for reasons for – the pros; the other half is reasons against – the cons. Where possible, a pro should have the corresponding con (if there is one) opposite.

What using the balance sheet method does is bring the conflicting thoughts whirling in our minds out onto paper. That way, we are less likely to forget anything important and we can stand back and look at the whole. With problem solving and decision making, the ability to stand back and be dispassionate about even (especially!) the most emotional of decisions is paramount. It truly distinguishes the professional from the amateur. The balance sheet method is a very simple aid to dispassionate problem solving which has been used for years, particularly by salespeople to get clients to make a decision. The decision should not be based on the number of pros and cons; it is the combined weight of those pros and cons or the criticality of certain of them which matters. Problem solving and decision making will never be easy; that is why we need managers. However, the balance sheet method can make their jobs much easier.

TABLE 23.1 THE BALANCE SHEET METHOD

Decision A

Reasons Against:	Reasons For:

Decision B

Reasons Against:	Reasons For:

How to make the best decision using the balance sheet method

Michèle, assistant to Emile Ratón, the world famous professor of methodology (see 22 The decision tree), was conducting a career development workshop with female managers, one of whom was called Gwen. It was quite obvious from their first meeting that Gwen was in a quandary about her career. Michèle arranged to sit down with her and explore the problems and alternatives in a series of structured sessions. One option being considered by Gwen was studying for an MBA. Consequently they drew up a balance sheet for a full time MBA, part of which is shown in Table 23.2. They also drew up balance sheets for a part time MBA, for a job change and for the 'do nothing' option – Gwen remaining where she was. 'Although I'm damned if I'm going to do that,' she sobbed. 'Put it down anyway,' Michèle suggested. 'That way, you'll know that you've explored all of the alternatives and done a good professional job.' 'I suppose you're right,' Gwen agreed, wiping her cheeks with a somewhat grubby handkerchief.

TABLE 23.2 AN EXAMPLE OF THE BALANCE SHEET METHOD

Decision A:	Take Full Time MBA
Reasons Against:	Reasons For:
Cost of course, expenses, etc	Greater marketability
Forefeited earnings	Access to more senior posts
Time taken after course to secure another job	Enhanced earnings
Disruption to family/social life	Wider professional contacts
Unfamiliarity with studying	Widened horizons

When all of the first and second order opportunity costs and benefits (see 24 Opportunity cost/benefit), had been worked out, all of the options collated and all of the balance sheets drawn up, it was time for Michèle to help Gwen to review the balance sheets. This proved a long and arduous exercise, which would have been much longer (indefinite?) without the benefit of a structured approach. And the conclusion? Well, that must remain a secret between Michèle and Gwen. Suffice to say that Gwen herself was considerably surprised by it. 'I suppose I shouldn't be; it's what I've always wanted, deep down inside. But if I hadn't followed a structured approach, I'd never have made the right choice. Doing it this way means that I know I've made the right choice in the right manner!'

Reference
Labaree, L.W. (1959), *The Papers of Benjamin Franklin*, New Haven: Yale University Press.

■ 24

Opportunity cost/benefit

■ *How to pick opportunities*

In management, decisions must be made. Because resources will nearly always be limited, there will tend to be competing demands for such resources. Should we employ them in this direction or that direction? Investment appraisal can help us evaluate the financial consequences of competing decisions. So can opportunity cost/benefit. Ideally, opportunity cost/benefit can be used in conjunction with investment appraisal.

Opportunity cost is the cost incurred by taking one opportunity as against another. For instance, in the greatly simplified example shown in Table 24.1, the opportunity cost of taking opportunity A is the forfeit of benefit B, which could have been secured by taking opportunity B – which, let us say, is no longer possible.

Opportunity benefit is, as it suggests, the benefit from taking an opportunity. But there can be a first order benefit and a second order benefit – and, for that matter, a third order of opportunity benefit. In the following example, we shall illustrate first and second order opportunity benefits.

TABLE 24.1 OPPORTUNITY COST/ BENEFIT

Opportunity A

Cost of taking opportunity A	=	Forfeit of benefit from taking opportunity B, i.e. benefit B.
Benefit of taking opportunity A	=	Benefit A.

Opportunity B

Cost of taking opportunity B	=	Forfeit of benefit from taking opportunity A, i.e. benefit A.
Benefit of taking opportunity B	=	Benefit B.

How to pick opportunities through opportunity cost-benefit

Emile Ratón, the world famous professor of methodology (see 22 The decision tree), was conducting a workshop with the directors of Calley Airlines when the vexed question of aircraft maintenance was raised.

'Yes,' declared Ratón, 'I have investigated your winter maintenance programme. And, if it has not been created by God herself, I must say that it is what you call absolute hogwash.' The engineering director of Calley Airlines glared at Ratón with hatred. Michèle, Professor Ratón's assistant, smiled serenely.

The managing director of Calley fought to suppress a grin. He gestured at Ratón. 'Now, Emile, why do you say that?'

'I say that because your winter maintenance programme is, how you say, "back to back", there is no room for error. And, from what I have seen going on – and not going on – in your hangars I would suggest that there is considerable error. Thus I conclude that this winter maintenance programme will not come to pass – at least not in the manner indicated.'

He flung the offending printout onto the boardroom table. The engineering director locked eyes with Ratón; Ratón gazed steadily back. 'Did it come to pass, last winter? Or the one before? Or the one before that?' he asked mercilessly. Silence.

'Now, these, what do you call them, these productivity consultants aim to address this mess with their systems and procedures and their development of people. What are they asking? A million pounds. And they will guarantee benefits of £3 million, principally through a decrease in overtime.'

'We could badly use that million pounds for new plant,' protested the engineering director. 'Which your people would abuse in the same way that they have abused the existing plant,' Ratón sternly retorted. 'So what would be the benefit of that plant? I will tell you, my friend. It would be nothing. Let us install new plant when we have developed the discipline to use it – not abuse it.'

'So,' he continued. 'Three million to one million. That seems like a good opportunity benefit to me – what our American friends would call a good deal. But that is only a first order benefit.' The board looked at him.

'Each day a plane is out of the air, you lose hundreds of thousands of pounds. If we increase productivity and improve throughput, those planes will have increased utilization.' He raised a hand to forestall the engineering director. 'Increased utilization in conditions of the same or greater, safety. For every extra day a plane is in the air, you will make about £100 000 extra profit. That, my friends, is a second order benefit.

'So, with this decision to improve productivity, there is a first order benefit, with a payback of four months and a second order benefit with a payback of one month. First and second order benefits – and, I admit, an opportunity cost with the plant not ordered or the interest that might have been earned from keeping your money in the bank.' At this, most of the board smiled.

Reference

Labaree, L.W. (1959), *The Papers of Benjamin Franklin*, New Haven: Yale University Press .

PART VII

Managing numbers

■ 25

Pareto analysis

■ *How to manage probabilities*

Pareto analysis is probably the best known rough and ready quantitative technique in management. Nevertheless, if you have not come across it before, here it is. And, even if it is familiar to you, don't forget that its uses are virtually infinite.

The example in Figure 25.1 gives a simple illustration of Pareto's Law. Of the items produced, some 20 per cent account for 80 per cent of the profit. Obviously, the other 80 per cent of items account for the remaining 20 per cent of the profit.

As with the normal distribution (see 26 The normal distribution), Pareto applies to practically every field of human endeavour. Roughly 80 per cent of accidents will be caused by 20 per cent of people. Roughly 80 per cent of your sales will be generated by 20 per cent of your salesforce. Roughly 20 per cent of your customers will generate 80 per cent of your bad debts.

Management requires – and will always require – control. Pareto analysis gives us a very good indication where we should be concentrating our efforts. Twenty per cent of your actions will tend to generate 80 per cent of your results. Fifty per cent of your actions will tend to generate 90 per cent of your results. There is no time to chase every paper clip. Pareto should be at your shoulder, guiding your every move.

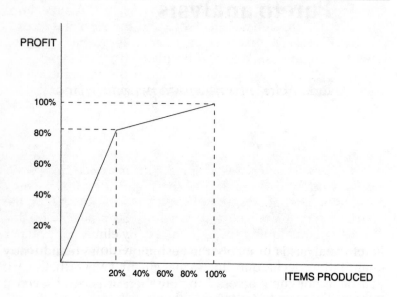

FIGURE 25.1 PARETO ANALYSIS

How to use Pareto analysis to make 20 per cent effort yield 80 per cent return

A certain factory was running with a large amount of production downtime. Consequently it had difficulty fulfilling its orders. Towards the end of a week and even more so towards the end of a month, the only solution was to authorize more overtime. Because overtime attracted premium rates, unit costs were pushed up. Consequently competitiveness was

suffering. Because productivity was low in the normal working week (bare time), shop floor bonus was depressed and
wages could only be made up through working overtime.
Continuous seven day working exhausted people, driving
productivity and bonus down still further and increasing the
costly overtime. A vicious spiral.

Some consultants were brought in to address the problem.
Initial reactions were sceptical. 'The problem is maintenance
engineering,' the consultants were told by everyone in production. 'We need a planned maintenance system.' 'Not so,'
cried the engineers. 'We've got a planned maintenance system. But we can't get enought time on the machines. So it
doesn't work. We're left with breakdown maintenance and little beyond.'

At the consultants' insistence, all production downtime was
logged by each machine centre, by cause. Histograms were
then produced and examined. In grinding, which was a bottleneck in the factory, 70 per cent of downtime came from waiting for work and through mealtimes, not through machine
breakdown after all. By running staggered mealbreaks on the
coiling machines, which fed grinding, 50 per cent of this
downtime could quickly be eliminated. By eliminating 50 per
cent of downtime in grinding, much more downtime further
downstream could also be eliminated. 'But why should we
have staggered mealbreaks?' the coilers asked. 'We like going
for our meals together.'

'While you lot are having your meals together, your
machines are switched off. And while your machines are
switched off, we're waiting for work. And while we're waiting
for work, so is the rest of the shop,' they were brutally told by
the grinders. 'Do you like losing your bonus and working
overtime?' The deal struck was that both coiling and grinding
would have staggered mealbreaks, thus reducing downtime
still further.

'This hasn't solved the problem,' the consultants pointed
out, 'but it does start to reduce downtime by doing something
which is relatively painless. We need to move through the
shop using Pareto analysis at each machine centre. And we
need to make sure that we're not looking at machine centres in
isolation. It's throughput in the plant which matters. We can't

solve everything at once and it's foolish to try. Let's use Pareto to indicate where we should direct our efforts. That's what it's there for.'

Reference
Price, F. (1984), *Right First Time*: Gower Publishing Ltd.

■ 26

The normal distribution

■ *How to manage statistics*

There is a sharp division between numerate and innumerate managers although I would claim that numeracy is de rigueur for all managers. But even among numerate managers, there is a sharp division between those who are statistically aware and those who are not. The demands of quality improvements, typically featuring SPC (Statistical Process Control), have increased statistical awareness – but usually only among production people. This is a pity as statistics can be useful for everyone. One of the most useful statistical concepts is the normal distribution, as shown in Figure 26.1 which applies to men's height in the UK.

The average height of men in the UK (i.e. the sum of all the heights divided by the number of men) is probably somewhere around 5' 9". The modal height (i.e. the most common height) is probably about the same. And the median height (i.e. the height where there are as many smaller men before it as there are bigger men above it) is probably also about the same.

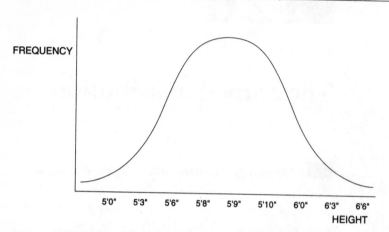

FIGURE 26.1 THE NORMAL DISTRIBUTION

If we now plot the frequency of men at different heights (either in feet and inches, metres, or percentages of the population), we will get a bell-shaped curve resembling a normal distribution. This curve will be symmetrical around the middle point. In other words, there will be as many men who are 5'8" as there are 5'10". Similarly there are as many men, (but much fewer), who are 5'6" as there are 6'. Again, there are as many men (but now, much fewer, who are 5'3" as there are 6'3". And there will be very few but nevertheless some men who are 5' and under and 6'6" and over. Because the curve is still symmetrical, there will tend to be as many 5' and under as there are 6'6" and over.

Obviously this curve, like all of the models in this book, is idealized. But, like the other models, it is realistic. Many attributes such as intelligence are normally distributed. With IQ, 100 is the mean (average), median and mode. Thus, we have as many people with an IQ of 85 and under as with 115 and over.

What practical use is the normal distribution? It gives us enormous predictive power.

How to harness the power of statistics using the normal distribution

Case Study 1

During a project in a financial services company, Harry Thayer, a section head, was asked by a management consultant how long it took to complete a corporate renewal.

'How long does it take us to do a renewal?' Harry Thayer repeated. 'That's a very good question.' He paused, looked pensively at the paper squalor of his office, turned triumphantly to the consultant and proclaimed 'Well, that's an impossible question to answer. It could take half a day or it could take two weeks. You can't really set a standard time for it.'

'I'm not trying to set a standard time for it,' was the level reply. 'I'd merely like to find out what is a reasonable time for a typical renewal.'

'But there's no such thing as a typical renewal,' Thayer persisted. 'So you keep telling me. Thanks for your help', was the seemingly disinterested reply.

That afternoon, a trawl through the timesheets revealed the times taken for the previous 100 renewals. Yes, five had taken less than a day while six had taken more than seven days. Twenty had taken less than two days while 18 had taken more than six days. Sixty-two had taken between three and five days.

Imagine Harry's surprise the following morning when he saw the renewal times plotted as a normal distribution, with two hours as a minimum time and two weeks as a maximum. 'Two hours or two weeks, Harry?' suggested one of his peers, pointing to the curve. 'Try four days for a start. And then let's see if we can get it down to three.' Harry's face was bright red – and not the blustery red induced by his lunchbreaks.

Case Study 2

After determining the capacities of different work centres in an automotive supplies manufacturer, internal work teams set about realizing throughput rates which would return their company to profitability and secure them a group bonus. For a particular large spring, the target throughput rate at tempering was deemed to be 200 per hour. A typical shift's production, where there was no downtime, read as follows: Hour 1 – 198 units, hour 2 – 200 units, hour 3 – 199 units, hour 4 – 200 units, hour five – 200 units. Imagine the suprise of the tempering team when their colleagues abruptly advised them to 'Quit the go-slow. You're robbing us of our bonus.'

'Oh no we're not,' was the defensive rejoinder. 'Oh yes you are,' was the equally vehement riposte. 'Take a look at your normal distribution some time. It's not a bell; it's a bloody needle.'

Ron Shadbolt, the tempering team leader inwardly groaned. He had thought that statistics was for window dressing and SPC idiots; not that it would remorselessly expose his little scam. When he further considered how much his lads and he had lost and how much 'them others' had gained through going from individual to group bonus he felt fit enough to howl.

Reference
Price, F. (1984), *Right First Time*, Aldershot: Gower Publishing Ltd.

■ 27

Zipf's Law

■ *How to relate frequency to rank*

Zipf's Law, like the much better known Pareto analysis (see 25 Pareto analysis), is a method of swiftly deciphering a pattern in what may, at first glance, seem like homogeneous masses of information. Zipf's Law states that where F is the frequency of something occurring and R is its rank, i.e. its relative order of occurrence (first = most often occurring, second = second most often occurring, etc .).

$$F \propto 1/R$$

In other words, the frequency of an item is inversely proportional to its rank. Thus the third most common word in the English language ranks third in usage, i.e. is found a third as often as the most common word. The hundredth most common word ranks 100 in usage; it is found one hundredth as often as the most common word.

The original work was done by a sociologist called George Zipf in the 1940s, counting the frequency of words in large

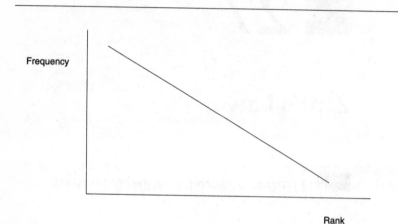

FIGURE 27.1 ZIPF'S LAW

quantities of prose. He found that the law seemed to be generally applicable. Thus in England the second largest city, Birmingham, is roughly half the size of the largest, London. Similarly, the third largest city, Manchester, is roughly a third of the size of the largest, and so on. The hundredth largest city will roughly be a hundredth of the size.

How to relate frequency to rank using Zipf's Law

Hugh wanted to set up a language training school to service learning needs in the York area. He quickly found that there were seven other such language schools in existence. Some were large and well established, others not so. Some were limited companies while others were partnerships and sole traders.

Hugh ranked the seven businesses in terms of size, as best he could. Finding out the turnover and profitability of the largest was easy as it was a limited company and filed accounts in Companies House. Using Zipf's Law, Hugh decided that the second largest company would have roughly half the turnover of the market leader; the third largest company would have roughly one third of the turnover, and so on. Adding up the turnovers of the seven gave the approximate market size. Doing likewise gave the overall profitability of the market. Hugh was now in possession of two highly interesting pieces of information. He had the overall market size and he had the relative market shares and their consequent profitabilities. Should he enter the market as the eighth largest language school, it was likely that he would have one eighth of the market share and profitability of the front runner. Was this worth working towards?

Hugh quickly decided that it wasn't. It seemed to him that, once you dropped lower than the third runner, being in the language school business in York wasn't worth the effort. However, a similar analysis of language schools in the Bristol area told a markedly different story. The combination of Zifp's Law and a particularly generous development grant had him packing his bags and heading down to the railway station. As the train pulled away, he silently toasted George Zipf with British Rail coffee. The nice thing about such a marketing technique was that it was as quick as it was cheap. The joys of the Minster paled beside the prospect of the land of Avon.

Reference
Zipf, G.K. (1949), *Human Behaviour and the Principle Of Least Effort*, Reading, Mass: Addison-Wesley.

PART VIII

Managing people

■ 28

Intrinsic and extrinsic motivation

■ *How to select experts and managers*

Given that much of management involves achieving results through people's actions, a great deal of consideration has been given to the subject of motivation. Everything else being equal, if people are highly motivated to achieve results, then management of those people will be a less demanding task than if they are poorly motivated. Thus the plethora of books about motivation, some treating the subject as a holy grail.

Another 'holy grail' managerial subject is leadership. Often books on leadership treat it as a separate entity from motivation. What is leadership if not the ability to motivate? Interestingly, the British Army's definition of leadership is 'getting people to do what they don't want to do.' (The premise here is that some things which people don't want to do – such as risking their lives – are, under certain circumstances, worthwhile.)

Still more discussion has revolved around whether or not managers need to be leaders. If management is about enabling people to achieve results and, people being people, either they need to be motivated or a climate needs to be maintained in which they motivate themselves, then a manager must be a motivator and thus a leader.

But many managers make bad leaders and thus bad managers. Often they refuse to think of themselves as leaders or even managers at all. Instead they may term themselves 'administrators' and hide behind the paperwork (or, nowadays, the screen) rather than facing the sticky, messy issues involved in motivating people. Meanwhile people learn to lose interest. The weak head teacher, the inadequate research chief, the ineffectual 'co-ordinator' – how much damage they can do.

So, managers are, *de facto*, leaders, not administrators. A good manager will inspire many, many people and be an inestimable asset to their organization; a bad manager should be helped. If help is futile, they should be replaced. Hard but not unfair. Who would be in favour of a surgeon or any other professional who was incompetent remaining in their job?

But what of the motivations of managers themselves? One, seemingly overlooked, way of looking at the issue of motivation is in terms of intrinsic and extrinsic motivation. Their definitions are simplicity itself. Intrinsic motivation is where I am pleased because of what *I* achieve; extrinsic motivation is where I am pleased because of what *my people* achieve.

Of the two, intrinsic motivation comes much more easily to most people. Pure experts, in any profession, are intrinsically motivated. But a manager must be significantly extrinsically motivated. They must say to themself, 'If my job is dependent upon other people's success then it must be their success which motivates me. My own intrinsic satisfactions are secondary.'

Many recruiters look for 'team players'. This is usually a gross oversimplification. Often, what they are really looking for, but haven't properly defined, is people with genuinely extrinsic motivation, people who will be unselfish enough to sacrifice intrinsic satisfactions to extrinsic demands. Such people are in surprisingly short supply. Think of the managers you know. Do they do what they *like* doing (intrinsic motivation) or what *needs doing* (extrinsic motivation)? If it's the former, they will make bad leaders; if the latter, they will make good ones. Industry, commerce and the public domain have had generations of bad leaders; those can no longer be afforded.

How to select experts and managers by using intrinsic and extrinsic motivation

Selecting experts is relatively easy. Assuming they have the necessary skills, and the determining factor between different candidates is motivation, all that one is interested in is intrinsic motivation. If the candidate is going to be spending their working life performing skilled operations alone at a VDU, then what does it matter if they are not a team player? They are not being asked to play a team game. They may be a maverick or a prima donna. Their manager may have to integrate the activities of a whole host of prima donnas, in which case the last thing the manager can afford to be is another prima donna. We are looking for intrinsic motivation, in other words, we are looking for evidence of delivery of results in the chosen area. If we are taking on trainees then have they delivered results in any area?

With managers, it is much more difficult. Nearly always, their early work will have relied upon intrinsic motivation. The engineering manager was once an engineer, the head teacher was once a teacher. Were they motivated when motivation was intrinsic? If not, then abandon them – management is not an easy option along the lines of 'those who can, do; those who can't, manage'.

So the first hurdle is intrinsic motivation. If the person was intrinsically motivated then search for evidence of the difficulty they had in becoming extrinsically motivated. If you find no evidence of such difficulty then again abandon them. (Alternatively you may be in the presence of a superperson – no, don't take the risk!) The supervisor who tore himself away from the delights of machine setting, the super saleswoman who trained herself to become an outstanding sales coach (and achieved the results to prove it), the technical director who is not just another boffin – these are to be prized and cherished.

Who are not to be prized and cherished? The technical director who goes to the Receiver for an increase in his budget is obviously operating from intrinsic not extrinsic motivation. So is the managing director of a troubled management consultancy who spends 30 per cent of his time abroad running management development courses because 'I like doing it.'

In many organizations, the only route to promotion and status is a managerial one. This is corporate suicide. The organization ends up with professionals who are managers only for the money and the status. In truth, they are not managers at all. Better to free such managers to be good experts (if they can be), rather than poor managers. The feeble department head in a financial services firm who went back to being a superb investment analyst with no loss of earnings or status; the sales manager who went back to being the top salesperson; the management consultancy director who went back to being a practising consultant – all of these were people who were helped to exchange a managerial extrinsic motivation which they did not want for a professional intrinsic motivation which they did. We are all good at something ... Managers need to be skilled at creating and maintaining environments where peoples' talents are best used for the organization's sake and theirs. Necessary; never easy!

■ 29

The managerial grid

■ *How to manage people and tasks*

The managerial grid addresses two elements of management – the ability to manage relationships with people and the ability to get things done (task orientation). People orientation is given a score from 1 to 10; task orientation is also given a score from 1 to 10. Each manager completing the grid is asked to assess himself or herself in terms of these dimensions. The mulitplicand then locates their position on the grid. Taking extreme positions in the four quadrants, we have the following possibilities:

Country Club management (1.9.): the manager fosters great relationships with the staff. Everyone is happy; very little gets done.

Ghenghis Khan management (9.1.): things get done because Ghenghis is a harsh taskmaster. But who wants to work for Ghenghis? Pretty soon absenteeism will soar as people feverishly apply for jobs elsewhere. And then things definitely won't get done; apart from Ghenghis, there will be no-one left to do them.

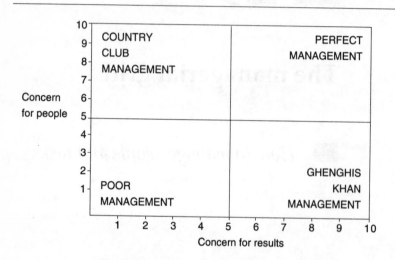

FIGURE 29.1 THE MANAGERIAL GRID

Poor management (1.1.): here, the incumbent is poor both at managing relationships and at task accomplishment. A career change is perhaps called for.

Perfection (10.10): the only person I ever met who achieved a perfect score of 10.10 was a sales office supervisor who turned out to be an unmitigated disaster!

A more likely possibility exists: Middle of the road (5.5. or thereabouts). Is this level of mediocrity acceptable today? Does the individual want to improve and can management development help them to become a 6.6., then a 7.7., then an 8.8.?

How to manage people and tasks using the managerial grid

Andrew Newton was an atypical social services manager. Originally an engineer, he had as some put it 'discovered a social conscience', gone back to college to study psychology and sociology, remained at college for further professional training and started a career in social work. A quick mind and an eye for organizational detail resulted in a speedy promotion to manager. Before long however, people started to wonder whether it was a promotion too far.

'Andrew has the ability; he'll go a long way,' was the opinion of the director of social services. Tina Mason, the sector 5 team leader, was less enthusiastic. 'Andrew's bright, all right. He's a whizz with logistics. But he's bloody awful with people. I heard that Ruth ran out of a meeting in tears last week. Nobody wants to work for him; I certainly don't,' she stressed.

'It seems strange to have a social work manager who can't seem to get on with people,' Ralph Ellison, the head of management development, ruminated. 'What was he like, I wonder, when he was a social worker?' Several phone calls later he had his answer.

'Frankly, Andrew was brilliant when it came to sorting out the paperwork for his clients. But he was hopeless when it came to addressing more intangible needs. To be honest, I was delighted when he got promoted.' At this, Ralph ruminated further. Something would have to be done – and quickly, before that idiot of a social services director started interfering.

A management development session which Ralph himself ran two weeks later provided an ideal venue. It came as little surprise to Ralph, if not the other participants, when Andrew scored 8.3. on the managerial grid to Tina's 4.7. The other four people in the group scored similarly to Tina. All of the six people looked suitably embarrassed.

'Andrew was once an engineer – and a very good one by all accounts,' Ralph began. 'Engineers have to work to tight deadlines. Once the cement is mixed, it has got to be used. Every hour a project is overdue, the profit is eroded in savage penalties. Engineers have to be task oriented; I think we should respect that. Without engineers, our world would rapidly become uninhabitable.

'Social services personnel work in social services because they value people and relationships. Their people skills may help them as professionals and as managers. But management of social services – management of anything – requires steel. Andrew has got enough steel to build the Humber Bridge. But the rest of you...

'So who's right and who is wrong? Irrelevant. You're here now and you have to learn from each other. Andrew must learn that ultimately you won't succeed in spite of people; you'll only succeed if relationships are sound enough. The rest of you need to learn that relationships can be too cosy. It's a hard world out there and it's a hard world in here. Flaubert said that you don't make great art from good intentions and you'll find that we can't run social services on good intentions either. Whatever we do, we can't suit everyone. Choices, sometimes hard choices, have to be made. All of us care enough about people to be here. If we care enough about their welfare, surely we care enough to become sound professional managers. That means, goodbye Ghenghis and goodbye country club.' Ralph stopped, surprised at his unusual burst of eloquence. And then, equally unusually for him, he smiled. Only then did Andrew, for one, begin to feel better.

Reference
Blake, R.R., Mouton, J.S. (1978), *The New Managerial Grid*, Gulf Publishing Company.

■ 30

Meeting skills

■ *How to manage meetings*

Managers are paid to make decisions and implement the resulting actions. The normal forum for decision making is meetings. It might be argued that even individual decision making involves a meeting with oneself. Be that as it may, much managerial decision making is not individual but rather collective. Other people have to be present, must be involved.

Meetings probably waste more management time than any other activity. Even in the best run companies, most meetings are of dubious value; in less well run organizations, they are often a complete shambles. Those of us who have endured the mind numbing qualities of poorly managed meetings will readily testify to the resulting severe loss of motivation. Sitting in a poor meeting is like banging your head on a brick wall; it only feels better when you stop.

Many, many books have been written about meeting skills and the virtues of chairmanship. The model shown in Figure 30.1 views meetings in terms of input, content, process and output – what you put in, what the meeting is about, how well it is managed and what the results are. Many people find the model refreshingly simple – and therefore useful.

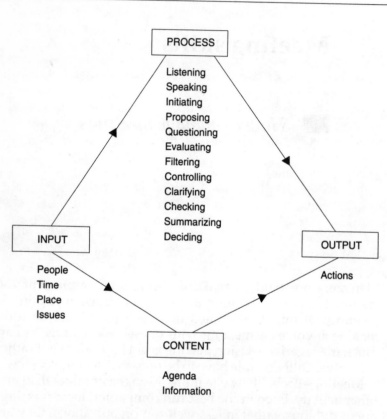

FIGURE 30.1 THE MEETINGS MODEL

How to manage meetings using meeting skills

It was the first morning of the teambuilding course at Grange Abbey. The previous evening had been typically fraught. At the opening session, participants had openly vied for position, such jockeying continuing unabated in the bar afterwards. Megan, who was running the course, had settled for a long run, a hot bath and bed.

This morning, autumn sunlight streamed through the great windows. Megan turned to her audience and grinned. 'You're probably used to learning by instruction because that's how you've learned at school and college. Well this is different. Most management learning employs experience – real or vicarious. My job is not to teach you about management; it's to help you to learn about management.'

'Let's take meetings, for example. Our first session is about meeting skills. Anybody here feel that they're pretty good at running meetings?' No hands went up. 'I'll prove to you that everybody in this room knows how to run effective meetings. You just don't know that you know.'

First they brainstormed ('though I detest the term,' said Megan) ways of wrecking a meeting – not letting people know, not having the room booked, not listening, not controlling the meeting, not progressing the agenda. And then Megan reversed the objections. 'So, if you're saying that if not having a room booked will wreck a meeting, then *place* is required. You're saying that if not listening will wreck a meeting, then *listening* is required.' And so on. When she had finished, they located the various requirements on an input, content, process, output model and ended up with the list shown in Figure 30.1.

'So we really did know how to run an effective meeting, after all. If we put these inputs in, address the content, work hard at the process and get the output, it won't be such a bad meeting, will it?' The participants looked at her, suspecting a trick. 'There isn't one,' she told them, thereby instantly acquiring an added reputation for mindreading.

'A few more comments. The inputs tend to cost a great deal – principally in management time. Don't waste them. A good meeting can motivate many people, including people not at the meeting – and *vice versa* – there are multipliers involved. Managing the process is the particular duty of the chairperson – but it is also a responsibility for everyone at the meeting. Different people are better at different parts of the process, such as evaluating, clarifying and initiating – this links with some work we'll be doing later about team roles. Hidden agendas – personal, illegitimate agendas – are explosive. Either address the hidden agenda directly or, usually better, rigorously exclude it from the meeting, if necessary convening a separate meeting. If the hidden agenda is not important enough to warrant a separate meeting being convened, then it isn't important enough to ruin this meeting – so forget it,' she tersely advised them. 'Lastly, make sure decisions are made, get resulting actions, and make sure people are accountable for them, with binding due dates. Meetings without actions are expensive holidays.'

She smiled wryly. '"By when" are the two most abused words in the history of management.' Her audience stared at her, agog.

Reference
Janner, G. (1986), *Janner on Meetings*, Aldershot: Gower Publishing Ltd.

■ 31

Team formation

■ *How to create an effective team*

Teams begin as groups which are, in turn, composed of individuals. The difference between a group and a team is that a team is a group united by a common purpose. The people in your train carriage are a group; they are not a team. If they joined together in a common purpose such as fighting off muggers, they would be a team. But how effective would they be? Unless teams successfully go through the following process, they are unlikely to be effective.

Forming: here we start with the raw material of a team – a group. Each individual has two passports as it were. One passport is the normal one – for instance, John Binns, engineering manager; the other passport is the group one – John Binns, member of the senior managers' development group. His first passport probably has considerable personal import; his second passport probably has not.

Storming: here the group members test both the group's

shared purpose (if any) and their pecking order in the group. In the process, they discover each others' attributes. This process of shared discovery proceeds through people engaging in conflict. Each individual has a bubble of personal space, identity, values and culture. They push their bubbles against other people's bubbles to see what prevails. John Binns is probably now using strong language and wishing he had never come into the group in the first place.

Norming: here the group starts to develop shared norms relating to their common purpose. Individual bubbles overlap into a collective bubble. A sense of shared purpose begins to emerge. John's new passport is becoming more important than his old one.

Performing: only now is the team able to work effectively upon chosen tasks. Up until now, there have been many embarrassing failures. Now the team feels that it is 'getting its act together'. All else being equal, the more thoroughly the team has undergone the previous stages, the more effective will be its task accomplishment.

Dorming: this is a stage of release. The team's mission has been accomplished; it is time to disband. Ironically, the sense of shared purpose is probably greater than ever. This is a time of grieving. John Binns cannot believe how much he cares for and will miss these people. Individuals will carry with them gilded memories of 'the way we were'.

Reforming: here the members return as a team. Although they may have to re-enact some or all of the previous stages of forming, storming and norming, this time the process will tend to be much faster and less painless. Omissions of some of the former members and/or the addition of new members will, however, tend to inhibit progress.

How to create an effective team through team formation

Megan, the course leader, surveyed the syndicate group on the first evening of the teambuilding session at Grange Abbey. Lucy was quiet, confident and highly numerate – a financial controller for a local industrial group. David, bespectacled and nervous, was a physicist. Damon was young and enthusiastic whereas Mark was somewhat of a 'fly by night,' she judged. Camilla, a buyer for a fashion house, was elegant, sophisticated and almost overwhelmingly confident. Paul was a hard nosed engineer and Jim was a stolid production manager. Anthea was an assistant director of social services. On the first evening, the group was really three sub groups – Lucy, Camilla and Anthea; Paul, Jim and David; Damon and Mark.

The next day was sheer hell, as Megan had known it would be. The group was rent by a power struggle between the hawks – led by Paul – and the doves, led by Anthea. Paul could muster support from Jim, Lucy and Mark while Anthea had Camilla, David and Damon storming with a vengeance. By the end of the day, the cracks in the respective leaders' power bases were glaringly apparent. It only awaited a late night defection by Jim, Lucy, David and Damon to create a middle ground – with the balance of power now firmly in the hands of the 'moderates'.

The morning of day two saw an attack from Anthea which drew a swift response from Paul. By now, both Camilla and Mark seemed more interested in flirting with each other than being ideological rivals. Invited by Lucy to 'Stop it, you two, we've got work to do!', Megan knew that the norming stage was beginning. With little resistance from the defeated leaders and dependable support from Jim and David, Lucy spent the remainder of the day creating a sense of shared purpose in the fast emerging team. Each completed task, each small success, was remorselessly built upon by Lucy as she welded her team into a force to be reckoned with. The odd outbreak of storming was ruthlessly surpressed by Lucy and her able lieutenants. By day three, the syndicate was performing so well that it achieved the highest score ever recorded in the Grange Abbey business game. When it was time for the participants to leave at the end of day four, moist eyes were in abundance – even from the likes of Paul and Mark. Progress, Megan quietly noted to herself, progress.

Reference
Adair, J. (1986), *Effective Teambuilding*, Aldershot: Gower Publishing Ltd.

■ 32

Team roles

■ *How to create a more effective team*

Most people chosen to be in a team are picked because of their functional expertise. A board of directors will tend to include, at least, a financial director, an operations director, a human resources director and a technical director – corresponding to the various functions in a typical company. But unless the board of directors works well as a team, little good will ensue. All their knowledge of finance and operations and technology will be of little use to the board if the directors do not work as a team. History is littered with examples of 'teams' entirely composed of prima donnas; almost always, they fail.

Functional roles are invariably necessary because functional skills are required. It is usually better to have an accountant as financial director, rather than as a human resources director. But functional roles are not the only roles possible for team members. The following team roles have been identified, corresponding to how people work together as a team:

Plant: the 'ideas' person. Bright, quirky, unconventional, impatient.

Shaper: the person who will take an idea raised by the plant, for instance, and mould or beat it into a more useful shape.

Monitor-Evaluator: the person who will say, 'Great idea. Now how do we make it work? The suggested expense is way over budget.' The idea will be tempered – or doused – by icy realism.

Resource-Investigator: the person who will look outside the immediate team for assistance or support. Mr – or Ms – Fixit. 'I know someone who's just dying to invest. That takes care of your budget variance.'

Company Worker: the person who will unselfishly work for the team.

Chairperson: the person who will orchestrate the team and its roles.

Team Worker: the 'people person' who keeps checking on other people's feelings. Neglect this attribute and wait for the outbursts!

Completer-Finisher: the person who makes sure that the task is finally finished. Mr/Ms Details. No finisher means no finish.

How to create a more effective team using team roles

On the afternoon of the second day of the teambuilding exercise at Abbey Grange, Megan, the course leader, introduced the participants to team roles. She explained the concept and gave succinct examples of each of the roles.

'The way I always think of it,' she stressed, 'is the processing of an idea. The plant has the idea in the first place and the shaper turns it into a worthwhile form. The monitor-evaluator checks the resources needed for processing the idea while the resource-investigator goes outside the team, if need be, for additional help. The company worker keeps tasks progressing while the team worker keeps the team progressing. The completer-finisher makes sure that the team gets a result. The chairperson oversees operations and ensures that the team is synchronized.' Megan looked at the participants and smiled. 'Each of you will have primary and secondary roles – so you get two bites of the cherry. Assessment is quite simple – a self-scoring test. I have my own ideas about who's who – but let's find out for certain.'

Each member of the team completed the exercise and shouted out their scores to Megan, who logged them on a pre-prepared grid. To no-one's surprise, Lucy emerged as a strong chairperson and Jim came out as an equally strong company worker. Camilla, well used to dealing with all manner of outsiders, was a resource-investigator while David, the physicist, was a monitor-evaluator. Perhaps surprisingly, Anthea emerged as a shaper and Damon as a team worker. Mark was another shaper and Paul was another monitor-evaluator. 'So that's it,' Megan concluded. 'Eight of you and only six roles filled.'

'What about secondary roles?' Damon asked. 'Yours is a plant,' Megan told him, 'and you're acting like one, right now.' At this, he blushed furiously but his eyes gleamed with pride. 'Jim, you have completer-finisher as a secondary role. Like Damon, you're going to have to develop your secondary role in this team. A team which doesn't have either a plant or a finisher will almost certainly fail.' At this, Megan noted, Lucy nodded thoughtfully.

'So.' Megan surveyed them with satisfaction. 'A team of eight people with eight well defined roles. Learn to use them. And learn to cover if a crucial role is missing. Any person can improve on all roles; it's merely a question of becoming flexible. But use the integration of these roles as your strength – that way you will become truly invincible.'

The very next day, in the business game, they proved her right.

Reference
Belbin. R.M. (1986), *Management Teams. Why They Succeed Or Fail*, London : Heinemann.

■ 33

Role negotiation

■ *How to develop sound relationships*

Me	You
How I see you	How you think I see you
What I expect of you	What you think I expect of you
How I think you see me	How you see me
What I think you expect of me	What you expect of me

FIGURE 33.1 ROLE NEGOTIATION

Role is a set of expectations which people have of a person. A person occupying the role of a judge, for instance, is often expected to be dispassionate, scrupulous and stern, whereas a person occupying the role of a popular entertainer is expected to be none of these things. Imagine our confusion, our shock, our outrage, if popular entertainers became like judges and vice versa! Actors who become typecast find themselves trapped in a particular role which the public will not let them change. Our social identities are shaped by our roles; they are all-pervasive. In considering role and the power of role, three allied concepts are useful:

Role ambiguity: Here the person is not sure what their role is, i.e. what is expected of them. Role ambiguity is commonly found in organizations with poor induction, i.e. most organizations. Newcomers are unsure as to quite what is expected of them. Often, confidence plummets and the person psychologically retreats by finding another job (role ambiguity is probably the biggest single reason why people leave new jobs within a short time). Alternatively, people may forge their own roles, in which case, they may encounter a different problem – role incongruity.

Role Incongruity: Here there is a variance between the role as perceived by the individual and the role as perceived by others, e.g. dispassionate comedians, hilarious judges. Many 'problem people' in organizations are suffering from role incongruity if not role conflict.

Role conflict: Here there is a conflict between two or more different roles. A female supervisor, for instance, may experience role conflict between the expectations of colleagues (commitment to the company) and the expectations of her husband (dinner on the table).

How to develop sound relationships through role negotiation

'Nowadays, we use the words "job" and "role" interchangeably,' Megan, the course leader, pointed out in a Health Authority workshop. 'In so doing, I think we dilute both words.' She paused. 'I think it is best to regard "job" in terms of task demands such as "can this person diagnose measles and deliver babies?". Role refers to interpersonal demands and tends to be more situational. The role of a general practitioner in certain practices demands openness, collaboration, and active involvement in community affairs whereas, in other practices, it demands being a much more status conscious expert who must be deferred to.' At this, a ripple of appreciation ran through the room.

'This morning we have two groups – medical staff and administrative staff. James, from the medical side, and Sally, from the admin side, have agreed to be our subjects. James has previously written down how he sees Sally in her professional role and how he thinks she sees him. Sally has responded likewise. Each perception is in terms of three adjectives.'

Megan took the first card, looked once at her expectant audience and read, 'James sees Sally as "bureaucratic, interfering and imposed" whereas he feels Sally sees him as "compassionate, committed and vociferous". Sally actually sees James as "a maverick, financially irresponsible and aloof" and she feels he sees her as "professional, concerned and disciplined".'

Megan looked up from the cards, surveyed her rapt audience and declared, 'I think we should congratulate James and Sally for being so honest, don't you?' A first hesitant clap was reinforced by others, until a somewhat embarrassed Sally and James were drowned by applause.

'Clearly, if we stay here however, Sally and James will not work effectively together. Instead, they will be blocked at an interpersonal level – with adverse consequences for all of us.' Megan surveyed the group – the two groups. 'And it's not just James and Sally, is it?' she quietly asked. People shook their heads and murmured assent.

'What James and Sally have to do is negotiate roles which work for them – and us all,' she added. 'I'm here to help them. and we're all here to learn. We have achieved the first level of comprehension – how James and Sally view each other professionally. Let's go to another level – what they expect each other to do and what they each think the other expects them to do. Let's get behavioural!' At this, they groaned. 'Yes!' she responded, 'you've heard it before and you'll hear it again. The only worthwhile change is behavioural change.'

Several hours later, when James had promised to finish his budget work on time and Sally had agreed to stop continuously interrupting in meetings (with a penalty box for backsliding!), it seemed to the audience that progress was being made. Over the following days, weeks and months, Sally, James and many other figures from differing sides of 'the great divide' learned to negotiate roles which boosted their effectiveness and ultimately led to professional harmony.

Reference
Luft, J. (1984), *Group processes. An introduction to group dynamics*, Palo Alto, California: Mayfield Publishing Company.

■ 34

Assertiveness

■ *How to manage conflict*

Conflict is a natural part of our human condition. All people have similarities and all people have differences. Our differences as people guarantee that there will be differences between people. Different people have differing perceptions of the same event. For us, our perceptions are reality. Differing realities invariably conflict.

Conflict is inevitable in organizations, work and otherwise. It is of prime importance to managers. Conflict can be healthy or unhealthy but if it is not well managed, it festers. Unhealthy conflict blocks organizations. The 'Berlin Wall' between production and sales; the sign that says 'Maintenance Engineering: No entry'; the two operators on the night shift who won't speak to each other; the staff in despatch and the directors in the boardroom who will hardly be civil to each other.

At its simplest, conflict is a disagreement between two people. It can be represented thus:

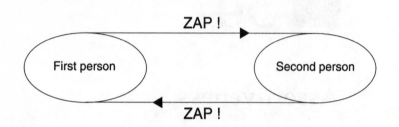

FIGURE 34.1 INTERPERSONAL CONFLICT

The danger with such conflict is that it becomes ever more personal and the original issue becomes irrelevant or overridden. Conflict of this nature cannot be resolved; the best that the participants can do is cope with it. Organizations are full of people coping with unresolved, festering conflict. Managers, however, are not paid to cope with problems; they are paid to resolve them.

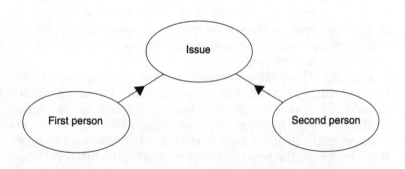

FIGURE 34.2 ASSERTIVENESS AND ISSUE RESOLUTION

In Figure 34.2 the two people accept that there is an issue about which they are in conflict. They accept that such conflict is natural; there is no blame attached. They contract not to attack each other, not to let the conflict become 'personal'; further, they contract to work together on the issue to resolve it for their mutual benefit. The participants have decided upon assertiveness as a mode of mutual problem solving. Assertiveness is not about attacking the person; it is about resolving the issue – for everyone's benefit.

How to manage conflict using assertiveness

'I think you'll agree that we have had our fair share of conflict over the last couple of days,' Megan, the course leader, mischievously suggested to her audience on the last day of the teambuilding session at Abbey Grange. There was a groan of assent from the course participants. Inwardly she smiled. Two days before, they had hardly been speaking to each other; yesterday they had been at each others' throats.

At its simplest, conflict involves one issue of difference between two people. If the people allow the issue to become 'personal' – or, more accurately, interpersonal, they will get pushed wider and wider apart. Typically, they will employ one or more of the following tactics:

Aggression: They will overtly attack each other.

Manipulation: They will covertly attack each other.

Capitulation: One will give in.

A typical combination is capitulation followed by manipulation, a ploy commonly employed by professional victims. There are four and four only possible outcomes to such tactics:

1. I win; you lose.
2. You win; I lose.
3. I lose; you lose.
4. We win.

Outcome 1 will lead to outcome 2, when the defeated adversary gets their own back next time – and vice versa. Aggression, manipulation and capitulation can only lead to outcome 1 or 2, and thus, inevitably, to outcome 3 overall. Ultimately, everyone suffers.

The only way to resolve conflict is to consciously aim for outcome 4, to deliberately decide to employ assertiveness rather than aggression, manipulation or capitulation. With assertiveness, we work on the issue – even (especially!) when the issue is interpersonal. Assertiveness means that we stand outside our problems and dispassionately examine them.

To make assertiveness work in practice, we need at least three conditions:

Mutual respect: The participants must respect other people – which means respecting yourself – enough to eschew aggression, manipulation or capitulation.

Legitimate disagreement: They must accept disagreement as natural and inevitable.

Psychological contract: They must contract to work on the issue for mutual resolution and mutual benefit.

'So that's assertiveness – in principle,' Megan smiled. 'There are endless different varieties and techniques – but never forget the philosophy and the principles or the techniques will be useless at best and counterproductively manipulative at worst. Now, what we need is plenty of practice!'

Reference
Gillen, Terry (1992), *Assertiveness for Managers*, Aldershot: Gower Publishing Ltd.

■ 35

The Johari Window

■ *How to find out what your best friend won't tell you*

The Johari Window considers communication between two or more people in terms of what is and is not shared. The theory is that true communication, for example mutual understanding, is only possible through shared knowledge. Often, in personal interraction, shared knowledge is drowned by knowledge which is unilateral and hence unshared. The Johari Window has four quadrants. These are as follows:

The Open arena: Here, what I know about myself is also known by other people.

The Blind arena: Here, other people know things about me about which I am ignorant. They don't tell me.

The Hidden arena: Here I hide things, which I know about myself, from other people.

The Closed arena: Here there are things about me to which both I and other people remain oblivious.

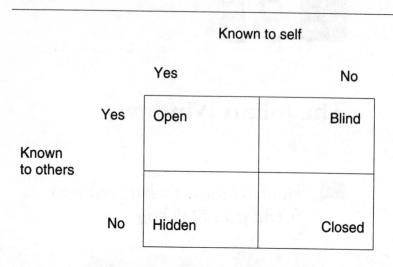

FIGURE 35.1 THE JOHARI WINDOW

How to find out what your best friend won't tell you using the Johari Window

'I've explained the basic principle of the Johari Window,' Megan, the course leader, said on the evening of the second day of the teambuilding course at Abbey Grange. 'But really it runs much deeper. If two people are truly communicating, then the only arena which they can use is the open arena of each – for only with open/open communication is there genuine mutual understanding. Unfortunately, their communication will often be jeopardized by thoughts which are hidden and behaviour which is blind. With two people who have interpersonal problems, the open arenas may be dwarfed by the hidden and blind ones.

'With three or more people, the situation may get much worse. Something about which I am – or would be – open with you, may be kept hidden from a third party. In teams which are interpersonally blocked, the collective open arena may be minuscule while mixed messages will be flying around. If true communication – mutual understanding as distinct from mutual misunderstanding – is impossible, then what chance does the team have of making good decisions and implementing them?' At this, Megan noticed with satisfaction, her audience was thoughtfully silent, perhaps reflecting how dependent our lives are upon unseen teams of people who cannot even communicate properly.

'So what is the answer? Well, one solution is total openness. Unfortunately,' Megan continued, 'this doesn't work. We will always hide things from other people (hidden arena), they will always refuse to enlighten us about ourselves (blind arena) and there will always be things about ourselves about which both we and they will remain unconscious (closed arena). Why is this? Probably because we find elements of life too painful and threatening to contemplate.'

'Total openness cannot and therefore will not work. A better approach is what I call "tactical openness", where we accept that, in many circumstances, miscommunication is in nobody's best interests. If that is the case, then it is best for people to be as open as they feel they reasonably can about the issue at hand. That way, openness proceeds, issue by issue. It's not general openness, it is specific openness. Although, intriguingly, specific openness, proceeding issue by issue, is often the best way to get general openness.'

'Enough of the theory,' Megan grinned.'Let's try a few exercises.' She began by using Lucy and herself as a learning set (this had been previously agreed with Lucy), while the others observed but did not interrupt. Megan and Lucy began a process of mutual disclosure where they started to open up first their hidden arenas and then their blind arenas. They started with relatively mild observations and then gradually increased the risk within limits which both considered acceptable. Before long, however, they were disclosing things about themselves and each other which even best friends don't normally talk about. Most members of the team were astounded.

'Johari is emotionally very, very powerful,' Megan stressed. 'It really does need to be used only between consenting adults – and at the right time. Facing the truth about ourselves, and knowing that other people know it, can be devastatingly painful.' She took a deep breath. 'But we need to learn to know each other as we really are – if we are to truly function as a team. If you use the Johari Window to achieve even tactical openness, you will be surprised at the difference in your working relationships with other people.' She smiled mischieviously. 'Try it and see.'

Reference
Luft, J. (1984), *Group processes. An introduction to group dynamics*, Palo Alto, California: Mayfield Publishing Company.

PART IX

Managing learning

■ 36

Spider diagrams

■ *How to do your own brainstorming*

Most creative people are highly divergent thinkers, adept at extrapolating from the particular (an apple has dropped on to my head) to the general (there is a force of gravity). Conversely, most managers are sharply convergent thinkers, highly adept at going from the general ('I wonder what are the problems at Bloggs Engineering') to the particular ('Get me the P&L!'). Some few talented individuals are both highly divergent and highly convergent in their thinking – but this is truly rare. Consequently, few managers are markedly creative. That, however, does not mean to say that they cannot learn to be much more creative than they are.

Of the many, many methods for stimulating creativity, only one has become accepted and indeed enshrined in managerial ideology – brainstorming. Nine managers out of ten will have heard of brainstorming. Will one manager out of ten have heard of synectics or the Delphi method or...?

Spider diagrams are an individual method of brainstorming. They are blissfully simple. We start by writing down the subject about which we wish to brainstorm and then list each idea that occurs to us, drawing the ideas around the subject, as shown in the figure above. Each idea can become a secondary subject to generate mini ideas which can also be listed. The whole can later be arranged into a sequential order of idea 1 to idea 6, for instance. (As with conventional brainstorming, evaluation and placement of ideas into sequential order must come after idea generation.) Idea generation is divergent; evaluation and sequencing are convergent. Remember, in the creativity business, it is divergent first, convergent afterwards.

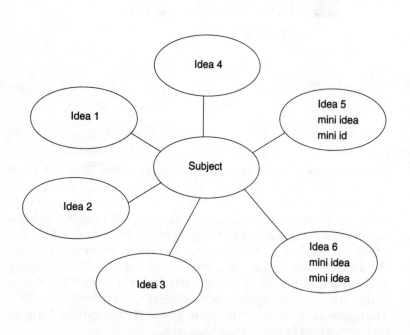

FIGURE 36.1 SPIDER DIAGRAM IN PRINCIPLE

How to do your own brainstorming using spider diagrams

Tamara had asked me to write an article about management consultancy for the business magazine of which she was editor. Accordingly I took 'management consultancy' as my subject and created a spider diagram – a web of ideas relating to the subject. The finished diagram is as shown in Figure 36.2.

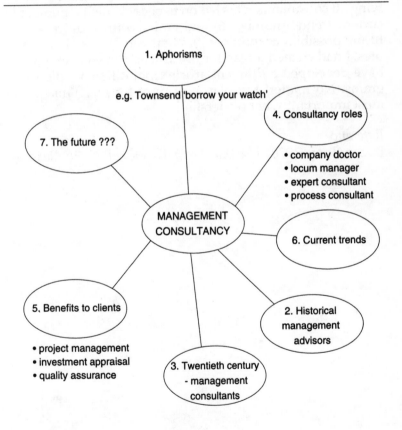

FIGURE 36.2 SPIDER DIAGRAMS IN PRACTICE

I simply started in the top right hand corner (because I like starting there) and worked clockwise (again, because I like working clockwise). When I had finished, I numbered the ideas in the sequential order which I found best. I wanted to start with an attention grabbing comment to arouse interest – so Aphorisms became number 1. Then some history, number 2, for perspective. After that, some twentieth century examples of management consultants seemed appropriate – number 3. An explanation of consultancy roles, number 4, would give my readers a simple and highly useful method of classifying all consultants. This led on to client benefits (number 5), current trends (number 6) and ended with a quick stab at future possibilities (number 7). What had I done? In ten minutes, I had created a plan for my article. Someone else would have developed a different article from different spider diagrams. No matter! My plan was right for me, Tamara and, most importantly, her readership!

Reference
Buzan, Tony (1970), *Use Your Brain*, London: BBC Publications.

■ 37

Key words

■ *How to speed read*

Key words are those words in a sentence, paragraph or page which contain most meaning, relevant to that sentence, paragraph or page. The simplest way to explain this is through a practical example:

'For many years, managers, academics and other business thinkers have conducted a vigorous debate about the relationship between pay and job performance. Obviously most of us come to work for money – but do we come to work only for money? What about the pools winner who continues to work as a plumber, or the heir to vast estates who works tirelessly in public service? And even when we do work for money, do we work entirely for money? Has job satisfaction no place in our lives? Even if we are well paid, will that guarantee superior job performance? The purveyors of self-financing bonus schemes seem to think so. On close examination, such schemes are usually found to be manipulated.'

This is an example of what I call debate-centred writing, where there is a continual interplay of argument and counter-argument. It is, thus, a relatively difficult piece to get to grips with. Let us try though.

We can summarize the first sentence in the following words: *business thinkers, vigorous debate, relationship, pay, job performance*. Twenty-two words have been condensed into eight key words. Obviously we could condense still further, but already we have cut down the number of words necessary to understand the sentence to about a third.

Similarly, we can summarize the second sentence into *work, money, only* – 18 words into three. The third sentence gives us *pools winner, plumber, heir, tirelessly* – 24 words down to five. Sentence four can be ruthlessly cut down into one word, *entirely* – 14 words to one. Sentence five gives us *job satisfaction* – eight words to two. Sentence six gives *well paid, guarantee, superior, performance* – 12 words to five. Sentence seven gives us – *self-financing bonus schemes* – 11 words to four. Finally, the 11-word sentence eight can be summarized in one word, *manipulated*. Overall, we have cut down a 120 word extract to 29 words. In other words, as long as we have a rough idea of what the other words are about, we can summarize the passage in less than 25 per cent of the whole. These key words are the words which we must learn to identify and concentrate our attention upon when we are reading; the rest are merely background. And let me repeat, this is a relatively difficult passage to reduce to key words.

How to speed read using key words

Hugh was a senior manager in a construction company. He had left school at 15 to become the bread winner of the family, when his father died. From a variety of shop floor jobs, he had worked his way upwards over a long time – nearly 40 years – to his present position. His rise had been characterized by qualities of determination, persistence and hard work – qualities which, he felt, were no longer enough.

'It was different in the old days,' he explained. 'You were a gaffer – you knew the lads and you knew the job and you just got on with it. But nowadays, it's all MBAs and discounted cashflows, that kind of stuff. We old ones just can't keep up.'

After spending quite some time with Hugh reviewing areas of personal effectiveness, one area we both highlighted was reading. Hugh's job entailed reading a large amount of technical documents, management reports and specially commissioned studies. In addition, he was expected to assimilate a wide variety of books and articles related to his profession. However, Hugh continued to read as he always had done, slowly and painstakingly peering at the words while following them with his finger.

The pragmatism of key words – that you only had to concentrate on one word in four or five – immediately appealed to Hugh. However, he had to learn to sit back, relax, and ask himself what the piece of writing was about and what he wanted to obtain from it. The example given above was obviously about the relationship between pay and job performance and it was written in a mildly provocative manner, designed to make the reader think about the issues from differing perspectives, for example, millionaire plumbers and stately heirs.

Hugh learned to relax, skim through a piece, highlighting key words and then to re-read the piece, only paying attention to the key words. He then had an effective précis of the text, thus ensuring that he never needed to read the entire text again. He could either put the piece aside as a précis (without any additional note taking) or re-read the key words. Even with documents to which he had to play close attention, Hugh found that he could highlight key words and read five times as quickly. Using the key words technique, he devoured his required reading, startling himself and everyone else. His final comment made it all worthwhile – 'I never knew that reading could be so much fun!'

Reference
Buzan, Tony (1970), *Use Your Brain*, London: BBC Publications.

■ 38

The behavioural learning cycle

■ *How to learn from experience*

Traditional approaches to Western education have focused upon learning through instruction. According to this principle, there is a strict division between the teachers and the taught. The teacher presents information, typically through 'chalk and talk'; the taught learn this information, principally by rote. Although current teaching methods are much more interactive, they have arrived too late to help generations of managers who have left school or college ten, 20, 30 or 40 years ago.

Managers are arch pragmatists. They are far more interested in experience ('the real world') than theory. And instruction is usually theory. Thus, instruction is not the best way for managers to learn; they learn best from experience ('the school of hard knocks'), either real or vicarious.

The behavioural learning cycle is a model of how to learn from experience. A piece of behaviour generates a result. To improve upon the result, we first need to reflect upon it (replay the video in our mind). We then need to generate concepts to hypothesize. What if we did this (new behaviour)? What would be the new result? How would it compare with the first result? Through generating, testing, discarding and ultimately selecting the most successful concept/hypothesis, we obtain the most favoured result. We then know which new behaviour is best. Our former behaviour is replaced by new behaviour; we behave differently. We have completed a circuit of the behavioural learning cycle.

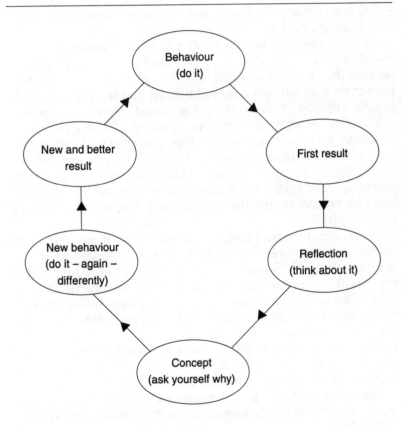

FIGURE 38.1 THE BEHAVIOURAL LEARNING CYCLE

How to learn from experience using the behavioural learning cycle

Simon had a problem. 'It's simple really,' he told me with disarming candour. 'To people in here, I'm God.' He gestured vaguely across acres of desalination tanks. 'To people out there,' he gestured across the wire mesh, 'I don't exist. Correction,' he rebuked himself, 'I might as well not exist.' He frowned, stared pensively at the doodles on his blotter. 'It didn't really matter before, when I was production manager; it matters like hell now that I'm general manager.'

Simon's problem was both simple and common – but no less daunting for all that. A modest and unassuming man by nature, he was shy, especially in groups of strangers. However, his promotion meant that he had to spend a much greater amount of his working life outside the familiar plant, often with groups of complete strangers. When he asked whether 'his condition was treatable' I assured him that it was.

Typically Simon would enter a group of strangers (behaviour), blindly head for the coffee stand, grab a coffee as a prop and doggedly guard the nearest pillar. If someone spoke to him, he would return the compliment. Usually they didn't (first result).

Simon and I worked hard on the reflection phase. What did he feel as he entered the room full of strangers? 'Panic,' he frankly admitted. 'Sheer panic!' What happened to his breathing (shallow, increased) and his pulse (quickened)? Did he take stock and look around him – (no!). What did he think of the strangers (nothing really). Did it occur to him (concept) that they might be as nervous as he was? Did it occur to him that it is impossible to panic when you are breathing slowly and deeply (concept)? Did it occur to him that you cannot be distraught when you are having fun (concept)?

Simon's new behaviour – calmness of posture, surveying the room, choosing his 'target', using a simple icebreaker, led to markedly improved 'second results'. In what seemed no time at all, he was 'working the room' like a seasoned professional – while remaining a highly capable manager and a courteous and gentle man.

Reference
Ward, Michael (1994), *Why Your Corporate Culture Change Isn't Working ... And What To Do About It*, Aldershot: Gower Publishing Ltd.

■ 39

The knowledge grid

■ *How to identify learning needs*

There are four quadrants to the Knowledge Grid:

Quadrant 1 is where I know that I know (something).

Quadrant 2 is where I know that I don't know (something).

Quadrant 3 is where I don't know that I know (something).

Quadrant 4 is where I don't know that I don't know (something).

How to identify learning needs using the knowledge grid

Jim Foss ran a factory, making components for the automative industry. The factory was based in a traditional industrial area in the north of England. Formerly, adjoining streets had resounded with the clang and whirr of hundreds of industrial processes in dozens of different companies. By the 1990s, there were empty streets, abandoned premises and rows of broken windows gaping at the sky. Jim knew that if he didn't initiate fundamental change in the way he ran his operations, his plant too would ultimately face closure. Yesterday's best just wasn't good enough.

	I know	I don't know
I know	Quadrant 1	Quadrant 2
I don't know	Quadrant 3	Quadrant 4

FIGURE 39.1 THE KNOWLEDGE GRID

Jim knew that new methods would have to be developed and learned. His forays into industrial training and development had left him confused. The knowledge grid gave Jim a method of beginning to assess his people's learning needs.

Quadrant 1 was simple. Jim knew that there was a significant body of in-house technical expertise, principally in metallurgy, relating to his industry. So far, so good. It would, however, be necessary to create a technical skill matrix and an allied training programme to achieve greater job flexibility among his workforce.

Quadrant 2 was also relatively straightforward. Jim knew that there were necessary skills which key people in his organization simply did not possess. These skills varied from European languages, to IT, to specialist matallurgical knowledge, to how to implement BS 5750. Again it was possible to relatively quickly pinpoint training needs and create suitable programmes.

Quadrant 3 was rather more difficult. Jim and I found that there was a huge amount of experience among his workforce which had never been properly utilized. Formerly, people had been employed for brawn rather than brain and managers had been highly autocratic; thus there had never been an emphasis on learning. Consequently, people didn't know that they possessed untapped in-house knowledge relating to technical aspects, production processes, process innovation, even how to run effective meetings. People had to be made aware that they had knowledge vital to their company's success. Their experience was a veritable goldmine.

Quadrant 4 was, and always will be, the hardest. Here people simply didn't know that they didn't know things – a condition of true ignorance. For instance, people thought that they knew how to plan. They regularly produced production plans, which were never adhered to. With difficulty, we got people to realize that planning is much more than the production of plans; it is a continuous, dynamic process. In a turbulent environment, planning becomes more, not less, relevant. Another instance – people didn't know that they didn't know how to behave assertively towards each other. The very concept and its importance were alien to them. They thought it was something 'bossy women learned to do'.

With difficulty, Jim and I worked to identify learning needs in quadrant 4 and move those learning needs to quadrant 2, i.e. where people knew that they didn't know. When assertiveness finally moved into quadrant 1, it was no longer viewed as anything to do with bossy women.

PART X

Managing yourself

■ 40

The Ivy Lee method

■ *How to manage time*

The Ivy Lee method, like most really good ideas, is eminently simple. When ideas are simple, there is a much greater chance of their being used. Anybody can easily use the Ivy Lee method to quickly gain much greater control of perhaps their greatest asset – their time.

Most people, even highly competent managers, squander their time by attempting far too much and being overwhelmed by a myriad of tasks. Often they should not be doing many of the tasks in the first place. Either the tasks don't need to be done or other people should be doing them (delegation). But managers who become drudges quickly end up as 'busy fools', working long hours and achieving little of lasting value.

The Ivy Lee method asks each manager to sit down each evening and simply ask him or herself, 'What is the highest priority objective for me to achieve tomorrow?' Let us assume it is 'Chair productivity meeting and gain agreement on cost benefits.' Thus 'Productivity meeting' becomes the first objective to be written down as an action for the next day. Our manager then asks himself or herself, 'Right, what's next?' and they perhaps decide that drafting a cost-reduction proposal for negotiation with a supplier is the next highest priority objective. This becomes the second action and is duly written down second. The manager continues until ideally six but perhaps five or seven actions have been written down. They then go home and forget all about them. If any further deliberation is needed, it is best done by the unconscious, not the conscious, mind.

The next day dawns bright and clear. The best part of the Ivy Lee method is yet to come! Our manager's goal is breathtakingly simple – he or she intends to achieve the predetermined objectives. Obviously time slots will, to some degree, have been filled. The productivity meeting will, for instance, have been arranged for two o' clock in the afternoon. Accordingly, even though this is at the head of the list, it cannot be accomplished first.

Incidentally, have you ever noticed that the managerial fetish about starting meetings on time is counterbalanced by a breathtaking insouciance about what time meetings should end? Every meeting should have start and finish times to which people should learn to adhere. If a meeting throws up other business – and most of them seem to – then it is often better to fix a supplementary meeting. Better many short meetings than a few lengthy, boring ones.

Meetings aside, everything will conspire to stop our manager successfully achieving one, never mind six ,of their objectives. This is the time for gritted teeth and persistence! Usually the more senior the manager, the more jealous they are of their time – because time is best used in the fulfilment of objectives. The Ivy Lee method gives such objectives.

One way or the other, the day will come to an end. This is the time for our manager to sit down, take out his or her list of six tasks and wearily wonder what the hell happened – sorry, I mean review plan against actual. The objectives which have successfully been achieved are struck off, the remaining ones go straight to the top of the next day's list, always assuming they are still relevant. The next day, we start again. We keep at it until we get it right. And then we simply continue with it.

A few points need to be noted. Most accounts of the Ivy Lee method are absurdly simplistic in the light of current managerial realities. It is easy enough to find six things you want to do; it is very, very hard actually completing them. A classic study, performed in the early 1970s, suggested that many managers operated within alarmingly short time frames – the hallowed figure noted was, if I remember correctly, seven minutes – just about long enough to have a cup of coffee and a chat. To managerially fill your day with many seven and sub-seven minute tasks is to become a busy fool. Better to complete few things well than have many half done.

To control your time, you will have to structure your day. The Ivy Lee method assumes sitting down at the beginning of a day to focus on the day's list and sitting down again at the end of the day to review the list and generate the next one. Such 'meetings with myself' at the beginning and end of the day are invaluable. Few managers have them; many managers regard the notion of meeting with yourself as some sort of aberration. Pay no heed! Meeting with yourself is the most important form of meeting you will ever attend. It truly marks the difference between the professional manager and the also-ran.

The Ivy Lee method does however have a glaring weakness – it does not distinguish between what is important and what is urgent. It assumes that important objectives should be attended to first. For this reason, I recommend that the Ivy Lee method is refined by using the priority grid (see 41 The priority grid). Adding only a little more complexity makes it much more precise. Incidentally, you will notice that most of the distractions of the day are urgent rather than important!

Another point – being firm with your time will require assertiveness, especially in the beginning. Better by far though to be respected as a professional than be regarded as an ineffectual nice guy. As a manager, you are paid to achieve results. If you don't have control of your time, you will not achieve results.

The original Ivy Lee method concentrated on 'tasks'. I have substituted 'objectives'. The easiest way in the world for managers to misuse their time is to spend it performing tasks – often tasks which their people should be performing (delegation). Certainly, some tasks will need to be performed by managers – and no manager should ever regard themselves as unworthy to perform tasks. But managers are, by and large, paid to achieve objectives through problem solving, decision making and implementation – and you will not achieve very many objectives if you spend all your time on tasks. So objectives, first and foremost.

How to manage time using the Ivy Lee method

The preceding section introduced the principle of the Ivy Lee method, discussed the practice, and mentioned some of the pitfalls. Perhaps the best example of the Ivy Lee method is the classic, athough possibly apocryphal, story of Charles Schwab and Ivy Lee. It is one of the few truly charming stories in the history of management.

In the early years of this century an eminent businessman called Charles Schwab headed a combine of American steel mills. One day he was visited by a management consultant called Ivy Lee. Ivy Lee asked what it would be worth to Charles Schwab if the productivity of his key executives were to be raised by 20 per cent. Schwab replied that he didn't know but it must be worth a great deal. Lee then offered to raise the productivity of Schwab's key executives on a payment by results basis. No results, no payment. However, in the event of results, Schwab would pay Lee what he (Schwab) thought the results were worth. A most gentlemanly arrangement, I am sure you will agree.

Ivy Lee then set to work to help Schwab's executives improve their productivity through the use of his eponymous method. After a respectable amount of time had passed, he returned to Schwab, who expressed his pleasure and agreed that productivity had indeed soared. His cheque was reputedly for US $25 000, a small fortune in those days. Client/consultant satisfaction indeed!

Reference
Bettger, F. (1990), *How I Multiplied My Income & Happiness In Selling*, London: Octopus Publishing Group.

■ 41

The priority grid

■ *How to determine priorities*

The priority grid provides a rational and structured way of determining priorities and consequently allocating resources of, for instance, money or time. It regards priority as being composed of two components – importance and urgency. In fact, it regards priority as being the multiplicand of importance and urgency, i.e.

Priority = Importance × Urgency

At its simplest, it is eminently suitable for managing time. With little effort, it can also be used to determine resource allocation in other areas such as budgeting.

Where there is a variety of demands, each demand is assessed subjectively on a scale of 0 to 10 in terms of importance and 0 to 10 in terms of urgency. Thus, something which was of maximum importance and maximum urgency (for instance, every member of a firm leaving the building at the onset of a major fire) would attract the highest rating of 100 –

top end of quadrant 1. Quadrant 1 would run from 25 to 100. Tasks of high urgency but lesser importance would attract scores of between 0 and 50 (quadrant 2) as would tasks of high importance and lesser urgency (quadrant 3). Quadrant 4 would attract scores of 0 to 25, reflecting low urgency and low importance.

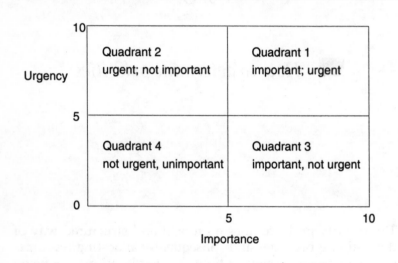

FIGURE 41.1 THE PRIORITY GRID

How to determine priorities using the priority grid

In my working with Henry to help him improve his performance at the Airline (see 43 The performance curve), one of the areas we looked at was how he spent his time. Thus I introduced him to the priority grid. He quickly grasped its principles. 'So one should do the tasks in quadrant 1 first, as they're both highly important and highly urgent. For me that would be something like preventing the maintenance system from collapsing. Next I should balance my time with important but non-urgent tasks like, devising an IT methodology to support our proposed planned maintenance system, and urgent but not particularly important tasks like presenting a paper on IT strategy at tomorrow's conference. I guess I should question whether I even need to do the tasks in quadrant 4 , like replying to unsolicited mailshots in which I have no real interest.'

'That's the idea,' I replied. 'Work through from quadrant 1 to quadrant 4, balancing out the demands of quadrant's 2 and 3. The scoring a particular task receives will help you but you will still have to make subjective decisions. For instance, you might have three tasks, all with scores of 32. But one task might be in quadrant 1, another might be in quadrant 2 and the third might be in quadrant 3.'

'So it's rational up to a certain point but I still have to make subjective decisions?' Henry queried. 'Yes. But we have to start from where you are at the moment. And, by your own admission, that's firefighting – doing whatever is urgent, whether it is important or not. While you are firefighting the urgent items, you're also firefeeding the less urgent items – they are simply becoming more urgent and stoking tomorrow's fires.' At this, Henry nodded thoughtfully. 'So don't expect to change overnight. You won't.'

Henry didn't change overnight – but change he did. Six months later he was in control of the most precious resource available to any manager and any human being – his time. The priority grid had worked.

■ 42

The effectiveness/efficiency grid

■ *How to be more productive*

In our lives, we have one sacred input – time. It is up to us how we choose to convert that input into personal outcomes. We can use the years to become chief executives, Buddhist monks, successful parents, circus performers. The choice is ours.

Management involves the successful conversion of inputs into outputs via a process of added value or added social value (see 16 The closed system). Whatever our prowess as strategic managers, ultimately we will judge ourselves by the operational criterion of how good a ratio of outputs to inputs we secure. That depends upon how well we manage the intervening process of added value or added social value.

Thus the primacy of the study of work and how to make work most productive. Notice that I say 'the study of work' rather than 'work study' which has, sadly, today become a devalued discipline. With the study of work, as with change, it is best to start by considering oneself, rather than other people. For this reason, the effectiveness/efficiency grid has been included under 'Managing yourself'; it is also applicable to 'Managing operations'.

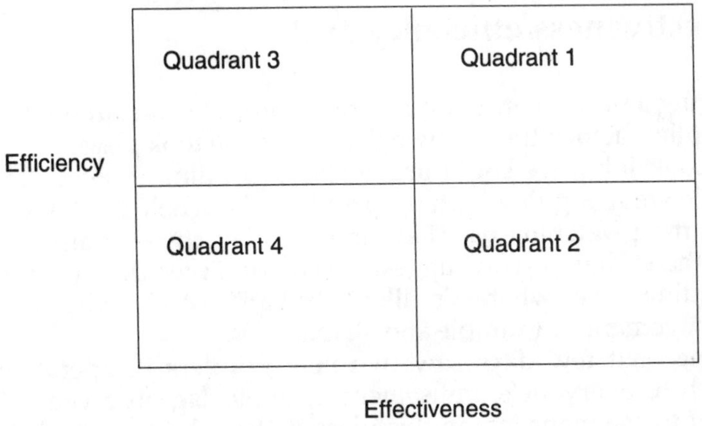

Quadrant 3	Quadrant 1
Quadrant 4	Quadrant 2

Efficiency (vertical axis label)

Effectiveness

FIGURE 42.1 THE EFFECTIVENESS/EFFICIENCY GRID

The effectiveness/efficiency grid recognizes the two components of work study – method study (what is the best way to do a job?) and time study (how long does the job take?). The fabled stopwatch may belong in time study; it does not belong in method study, which is far more important.

Quadrant 1 shows high effectiveness and high efficiency; work done here will be highly productive. Quadrant 2 shows work which is highly effective but with lower efficiency; training should be considered here. Quadrant 3 shows work with high efficiency but low effectiveness; job redesign should be considered. Quadrant 4 shows work with low effectiveness and efficiency. Job redesign is almost certainly the first step here. The aim of any worthwhile operational manager is to eliminate quadrants 2, 3 and 4. Only quadrant 1 results in truly productive performance. History tells us that even the best performance can and will be improved. If we don't do it, somebody else will.

How to be more productive using the effectiveness/efficiency grid

During a performance improvement project in an automotive supplies factory, the following conversation took place.

'Look John, we could argue about grinding forever. And while we're arguing with the grinders, the whole factory will be sitting watching us. That can't be productive for anyone.' 'So then what do you suggest?' 'Why don't we do a stint on grinding, see what it's like?' 'What?' 'Well, why not? Management by example and all that.'

The next few days saw two new grinders in operation, much to everyone's amusement. One old lag observed 'It's good to see managers in this place getting their hands dirty. Reminds me of the old times. And that consultant chappie as well. A bit of grinding will do him no end of good!'

After a couple of shifts John and I sat down to review grinding. 'Look at it this way, John. You and I are novice grinders. But our efficiency is higher than long serving grinders. And it's not us. When Eddie was transferred from upstairs, his efficiency was higher as well – until the grinders persuaded him otherwise.'

'But let's leave efficiency aside for a moment. Everyone around here is obsessed by it. The cult of the stopwatch and all that. What's inarguable is that effectiveness on grinding is pathetic. We're feeding the springs to the grinder with a shovel – very high tech! We drop springs on the floor, causing quality and safety problems. We dump far too many springs on the grinder and then can't move for springs. Even having a smaller shovel – or, better still, a scoop, would do wonders in the short term. The grinders don't insert the springs in a regular order; if you do insert them in a regular order, you can insert nearly twice as many in a given time – I've tested it!

'The list continues. Lost time for diamond dressing. Do we need to diamond dress so often? Let's run properly controlled trials and find out. No help from upstream or downstream, thus diminishing everyone's group bonus. No staggered mealbreaks, so a bottleneck is left standing idle. No job rotation on what is surely the most boring job in the plant. I'm sure that my efficiency on a two hour on, two hour off cycle would be much higher than eight hours working straight through – or, heaven help us, 12.'

'So what are you suggesting?' 'Let's work with the grinders to improve effectiveness. You've had my suggestions; let's ask them for theirs. When we have improved effectiveness, then let's see about increasing efficiency – but in a properly controlled fashion. Optimum efficiency is not necessarily maximum efficiency. Achieving the optimum multiplicand of effectiveness and efficiency is what will yield the best results. Effectiveness first; efficiency second. And the best result overall.'

■ 43

The performance view

■ *How to optimize your performance*

The performance curve isolates two variables – performance and anxiety. It states that, all else being equal, a person's performance will be a function of their anxiety.

At A, there is no performance and no anxiety. The person is asleep.
At B, there is poor performance and little anxiety.
At C, there is medium performance and low/medium anxiety.
At D, there is optimum performance with medium anxiety.
At E, there is medium performance and medium/high anxiety.
At F, there is poor performance and high anxiety.
At G, there is no performance but tremendous anxiety. The person is having a nervous breakdown.

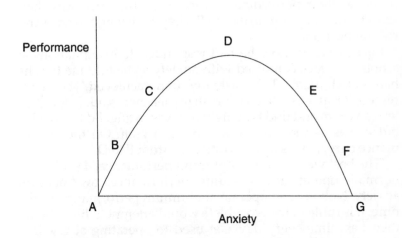

FIGURE 43.1 THE PERFORMANCE CURVE

How to maximize your performance using the performance curve

Henry was a senior manager in a national airline. He had tremendous responsibility and worked 16-hour days. When I interviewed him, he described himself, with great candour, as 'Managerially ineffective. I'm barely coping...'.

Henry knew that something had to be done. I explained the principles of the performance curve and asked him to locate himself on it. Unhesitatingly he located himself at F – poor performance and high anxiety.

Henry was dumbstruck when I suggested that he could probably achieve the same level of performance by operating at the low anxiety position of B. Although he found this morally unjustifiable, he reluctantly accepted the logic of the argument. I explained that highly motivated people like himself naturally shoot for D – optimum performance. But because of anxiety, they tend to overshoot and hit E, ironically reducing their performance. Very often this increases their anxiety and they slip further to F. They are trying too hard and risking burnout.

I asked Henry how he had responded to examinations at school. His face contorted with anxiety as he told me that he had hated them. 'I consistently underachieved,' he reminisced, 'or, at least, that's what all my teachers said. I would go into an exam and find that my mind was racing. I'd try to relax but it was as though I was fighting myself. On the performance curve, I was trying to struggle from F to D.'

'The best way to hit D – optimum perfomance,' I said, 'is to normally operate at C – medium performance, low/medium anxiety. Nobody can operate at optimum performance all the time; it is futile to try. No athlete would attempt to hit or break their best time every day. Get used to operating at C – it is much better than you are doing now, with a fraction of the anxiety. When you want to "go for gold", simply accelerate up to D and produce a performance which will astound your harshest critic – yourself.'

Henry and I worked together with specific behavioural techniques. In six months, the change was remarkable. 'Professionally, and perhaps personally also,' he confided, 'you saved my life.' Few accolades have meant as much to me.

Reference

'Yerkes-Dodson Law' (1972), Eysenck, H.J., Arnold, W. , Meili, R. *Enycyclopedia of Psychology*, London: Search Press.

44

The recovery cycle

■ *How to manage crisis*

The recovery cycle plots morale through different stages of personal crisis. Broadly speaking, it operates as follows:

A   This is the moment of crisis. Morale has been relatively normal.
B   If the crisis has been expected for some time (for example, the spectre of impending redundancy), there is often a temporary increase in morale – a sense of relief, of at least knowing the worst.
C   Such release, if it occurs at all, is strictly temporary. Once reality sinks in, morale quickly falls back to the baseline.
D   As the victim succumbs to shock and grief, morale dramatically plummets. If the crisis has not been anticipated, this will be the first stage – i.e. ABC, the release stage, will not occur.
E   From D to E, the person is in a state of grief. Morale may go slightly up or down but the person is very much 'bumping along the bottom'.

F   This marks a tentative stage of recovery. The person is coming to terms with their situation and realizing that life, although perhaps unpalatable, must go on.

G   By now, the long haul out of grief has been completed. Morale is about the same as A – pre-crisis. Barring occasional lapses, recovery is complete.

H   Often, although as with B not always, morale will continue to increase above pre-crisis levels. The person has successfully managed the demands of crisis and has emerged the stronger for it. With their new found strength, everyday problems pose far less of a problem.

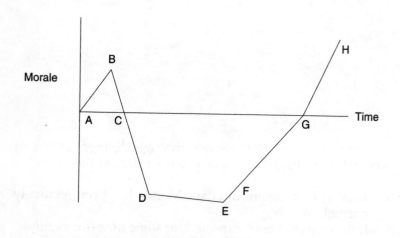

FIGURE 44.1 THE RECOVERY CYCLE

How to manage crisis through the recovery cycle

Aoife had been appointed managing director of a home improvements company, a mere three months before I met her. She immediately struck me as being more incisive than the rest of her board put together. Her long and arduous journey from the typing pool had been a triumph of dogged persistence over blatant sexism. So it came as quite a surprise when one morning, while discussing the problems of devolving budgetary control, she suddenly, and with no prior warning, burst into tears.

What can you do? Fortunately, there were only the two of us in an otherwise deserted boardroom. I proffered a tissue with which Aoife ineffectually dabbed at her rapidly widening streaks of mascara. I also silently waited.

'Oh, God, I'm sorry,' she wailed. 'What must you think of me? A typical woman getting up to a woman's bloody tricks. That's what they'd say.' She jabbed with her pen in the direction of the executive suite.

'It's my mother,' Aoife sobbed. 'She died six months ago – just before I was made MD.' She laughed bitterly. 'All those years of soul destroying work for a bunch of complete idiots. And my mother always pushing me, helping me, saying, "Don't be satisfied with what you've got; hold out for more. They'll try to grind you down; don't let them." But then she died – too soon to see the ultimate payoff.' Aoife's voice trailed off into momentary disbelief.

Besides immediate support and reassurance, Aoife needed some concept to make sense of her experience. We all need concepts to make sense of our experience – otherwise we remain trapped in it. I quickly and informally sketched the recovery cycle on the proverbial napkin – which was all we had to hand. Laughing through her tears, Aoife located herself at D. Although her life had involved a great deal of relentless struggle, Aoife had never before had to deal with such a sharp crisis. Inured to hardship, she was utterly unprepared to deal with such a situation. The recovery cycle was an instrument to help her do so.

'In acknowledging your grief, you've done the right thing,' I assured her. 'Most men and some women firmly believe that if they don't give in to their grief, it will simply go away. It won't. Denying grief prolongs the cycle – sometimes indefinitely. You don't want to spend all your life getting from D to E?' Aoife smiled wanly.

'In crisis, we are emotionally shocked. Our rational mind might say, "I've lost my job" and rationalize "Many people lose their jobs. My redundancy is no reflection upon my abilities. I have skills and talents and a track record. I'll work again." But deep inside we're shocked. So the subsequent stages of grief which we undergo are a necessary coming to terms with what has happened. If you deny the grief, you prolong the cycle. If you don't know about the cycle, you probably think you are falling apart.' I paused.

'What we must do in completing the recovery cycle is firstly realize that one day the cycle will be over and our normal lives can begin again. Secondly, we must compress the cycle so that our "downtime" is minimized – but we must responsibly compress it. That doesn't mean denial or avoidance. It usually means skilled help.'

With skilled help, Aoife moved through her recovery cycle in the following months. From her grief, she developed a strength at which her male colleagues could only marvel.

Reference
Littlewood, J. (1992), *Aspects of grief: bereavement in adult life,*
    London: Tavistock/Routledge.

PART XI

Managing change

■ 45

Organizational size

■ *How to manage organizational transition*

One of the least often considered yet most pervasive influences on organizations is, quite simply, size. The model shown in Figure 45.1 depicts three quite distinct stages of organization development due to size.

The Pioneer phase: here the organization is in its infancy. A pioneer has glimpsed a market opportunity (or, in the public domain, a social pioneer has glimpsed an opportunity or need). Management is *ad hoc*; there are few if any systems, and life is exciting or exasperating depending upon your view. Management is autocratic although vigorous protestations to the contrary are often made. There are probably between two and 150 people in the organization. Everybody knows everyone else.

The Systems phase: here there are probably between 150 and perhaps 800 people. The days of everybody knowing everyone else have long passed. There are the original people and the new people. Many of the new people are professional accountants, information technologists managers; their loyalty seems to be to their professions, not to the organization itself. Management is now much more dependent upon *role*, rather than personality. Team players are valued – sometimes to the exclusion of all else. The organization is in danger of drifting into becoming an unresponsive bureaucracy. The fun appears to have gone out of life.

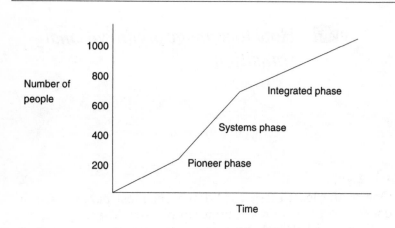

FIGURE 45.1 ORGANIZATIONAL SIZE

The Integrated phase: here the numbers of people in the organization, or at least on the same site, are approaching the 1 000 mark. The organization has become too large and too unwieldy to survive in the systems phase. Consequently, it has split into much smaller parts, mini-pioneer organizations, under a corporate umbrella. If this has been handled well (and it usually is not), the organization will have the flexibility of a pioneer organization yet the discipline of a systems organization – a truly enviable combination.

How to manage organizational transition through size

In a directors' workshop that I ran at the beginning of a corporate culture change programme, the following conversation occurred.

'We are a systems organization by virtue of size and complexity,' Andrew Kane, the chief executive, thoughtfully commented,' but we are a pioneer organization in terms of our culture.'

The other executives nodded their heads in agreement. 'That's the problem,' I concurred. 'On this model, which is surprisingly widespread in its application, there are three phases and thus, two transitions between the phases. We are trying to manage the transition between the pioneer and the systems phase. For years this plant has been subject to autocratic management. Workers were paid to do, not think, and were certainly not expected to care. They were paid for their hands, not their heads or their hearts.

'Because the company succeeded, autocratic management was deemed to be correct. But perhaps the company succeeded in spite of, not because of, autocratic management. Certainly, autocratic management meant layers of empty suits, policing the place, adding no value whatsoever.' I looked around. 'Today those layers are gone.' The men facing me nodded soberly.

'Before, we didn't need to be responsive to the marketplace – not with a waiting list for our products. Those days are gone. We now have to be infinitely responsive. Before, we did things because Fred wanted them done and Fred was in a position of power. The market advantage could support Fred's decisions whether they were right or wrong. Now we're going to have to do things because they are the right things to do. Instead of mavericks we need dedicated professionals – and teams. Before, we didn't need systems. Recently we've started to introduce systems – but does anyone follow them? I don't think so.'

'You're really saying that we need to make a radical shift,' Andrew suggested. 'I'm afraid so,' I agreed. 'But we have to be careful to keep the good parts of the past and not just have change for change's sake. I think we have to identify the good parts of the past and the ways in which we feel we need to change – and then begin a dialogue.' 'With the staff?' Roger interrupted. 'With everyone,' I bluntly told him. 'Not easy,' Roger observed. 'Some people around here have very entrenched attitudes.' 'It's never easy,' I pointed out, 'but we need dialogue, we need agreement and we need commitment.'

'What's the difference between agreement and commitment?' asked Roger. 'Agreement is when you agree to do something,' I replied. 'Commitment is when you have done it.' 'In that case,' Andrew drily observed, 'we've got rather a long way to go.'

Reference

Ward, Michael (1994), *Why Your Corporate Culture Change Isn't Working – And What To Do About It*, Aldershot: Gower Publishing Ltd.

■ 46

The principle of recursion

■ *How to manage systems change*

The principle of recursion states that, in any system, elements of the system (i.e. the subsystems) will evince the properties of the (parent) system. On this basis, we can represent an organization, the fictional Zenon organization shown in Figure 46.1 as an integrated system. Its elements, such as the marketing department and the production department, are subsystems. (For simplicity these are the only departments shown.) Order processing is an element of the marketing department and thus a subsystem of a subsystem.

Certain properties will recur, i.e. be recursive, within the system. Thus we will find them in the elements, subsystems and subsystems of subsystems. If the directors have ineffective board meetings then probably so will the department heads and so will the supervisors. If the receptionist is polite and professional, then it is likely the marketing department will also be polite and professional. If the van driver is helpful, then probably the technical sales representative will also be helpful.

Of course, not all people are alike. Individuals differ; so do groups. But an organization can be considered to be a social system – with its particular attributes – through and through.

The Zenon Corporation

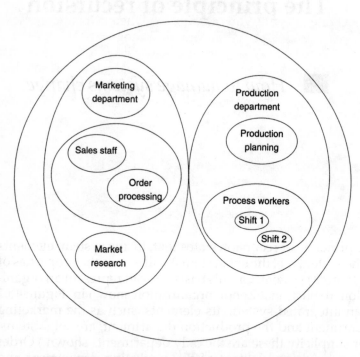

FIGURE 46.1 THE PRINCIPLE OF RECURSION

Managing systems change through the principle of recursion

During the directors' workshop I ran at the beginning of the corporate culture change programme (see 45 Organizational size), tempers were running high.

'Change!' muttered Roger Harrison, the production director. 'You'll never get these people to change. I don't care what you say. It just can't be done.' 'If it isn't done then we'll go out of business – as simple as that,' Andrew Kane, the chief executive, mordantly observed. 'We have to change – one way or the other.' 'I'll believe it when I see it,' Roger replied.

'The problem is,' I observed, 'that we can't wait for people to change. We have got to change them. And, in reality, you can't change people; you can only help them to change. One of the problems that people have with change is that it's always change for other people, not us. And yet we always feel that other people are different. They're not; really they are just like us.'

'What do you mean?' asked Roger. 'Well, you remember the principle of recursion?' I replied. 'I mentioned that you could very quickly understand an organization by identifying the conditions which were recursive. If the receptionist is helpful, then probably she's not the only one. If the foyer is stark and functional, don't be surprised if the organization is also stark and functional. Let's consider other people and ourselves in terms of conditions which are recursive.'

'You complain that departmental meetings are a waste of time. Well, how productive are your board meetings? You complain that people won't take responsibility and stand up for themselves. How many of you stood up to your chairperson when she was here last? You complain that people won't delegate. How good are you at delegating?'

'Well!' Roger practically shouted. 'There's nothing like paying people vast sums of money to insult you!' 'Hang on a minute,' Andrew cautioned, 'let's hear a bit more first.'

'If we want to change other people, we must change ourselves first. It's not just them, it is also us. They are affected by bad habits, viruses from the past. Well so are we. In changing recursive elements in ourselves, we will begin to change them in other people.'

'When can we start? We can start today, with ourselves. We can start by running decent board meetings. We can start by being assertive with each other – and with our chairperson. We can start by individually and collectively writing down what we do and what we should do and planning to delegate the difference. And we can continue by communicating these things to our people. In other words we make the principle of recursion work for us – not against us!'

Reference
Rickards, Tudor (1990), *Creativity and Problem Solving at Work*, Aldershot: Gower Publishing Ltd.

■ 47

The development of culture

■ *How to manage culture change*

The culture of an organization acts as a stabilizing influence upon day to day behaviour. Unfortunately, this stabilizing influence also acts as a counterbalance to change. Thus, most attempts to create change in organizations are doomed to failure because they do not address cultural issues. The most useful definition of culture is 'the set of assumptions implicit in behaviour' (Ward). Figure 47.1 illustrates the formation and maintenance of culture.

All organizations – a school, a prison, a hospital, a company – involve behaviour and results. Certain behaviour (for example, poor timekeeping) creates certain results (for instance, a blind eye – tacit acceptance). Within a short time, minutes, hours or days at most, conscious expectations will be formed that this behaviour leads to these results. If this behaviour-results-expectations cycle persists, then, in time, for example many months or perhaps a year, an attitude will be formed. People will be much less aware of the attitude (for instance, towards poor timekeeping) than they were of the

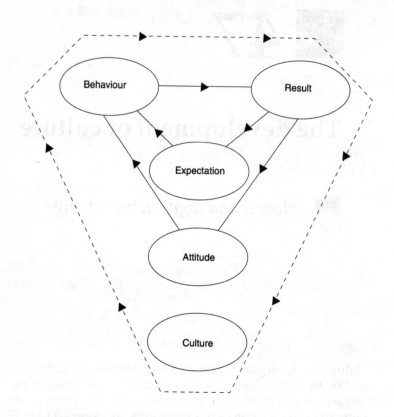

FIGURE 47.1 THE DEVELOPMENT OF CULTURE

expectation. With attitude, we are beginning to take things for granted.

Now we have a double loop cycle of behaviour, results, expectation and behaviour, results, attitude. Should the aforesaid behaviour and results persist then, in time, typically many years, culture will be formed. With culture, awareness is near zero. By this time, bad timekeeping is a way of life.

How to change organizations by changing culture

At the directors' workshop which I ran at the beginning of a corporate culture change programme (see 45 Organizational size), events were taking an interesting turn.

'Fine, Michael, you've explained how culture is formed. What you haven't explained is how we can change it.' Andrew Kane, the chief executive, looked at his board of directors. 'And change it we certainly need to do.'

'The problem with culture change,' I replied, 'is that managers think culture is something which can be switched on and off at will. It doesn't work like that. Culture arises over a long, long period of time. And it has its useful aspect in providing stability – stability which we all need on a day to day basis. So let's not look for quick fixes. There aren't any.

'It is best to think of culture as a mechanism which locks behaviour and results into place. As managers, what we want is results. To achieve results we need behaviour. If we attempt behavioural change in organizations we can fairly quickly change people's expectations. But their attitudes and their culture will act to counterbalance such changes in behaviour, results and expectations. If we try to directly change attitude and culture, we are focusing upon the derived variables not the deriving variables, and consequently we will fail.

'The best way to change behaviour, results, expectation, attitude and culture is to explain the above model to people. We then need to elicit attitudinal and cultural variables and see whether they are congruent with today's situation. I'll give you some examples of cultural variables in your organization which I think are incongruent. Many people believe that one man, one machine was right for their fathers and should be right for them. But some of your competitors are working one man, 12 machines. Similarly, many people believe that their earnings should increase, year on year, irrespective of productivity advances. But in a cost-down industry, productivity increases are necessary for survival and increases in earnings must be self-financing.'

I looked around me. 'We need to elicit these and other cultural variables, bring them out into the open and make people realize that some of their taken-for-granted assumptions about this organization are valid and some are distinctly invalid. We need to make progress on an educational front, get the arguments across to people.'

'At the same time, we need to understand current behaviour and results. The best way to do this is to interpose management control systems. We can then help people to use the systems to change their behaviour and results in a way which is congruent with what we are finding on the educational front.'

'Sounds like a twin pronged approach to me,' Andrew remarked. 'It's that and more,' I told him.

Reference

Ward, Michael (1994), *Why Your Corporate Culture Change Isn't Working – And What To Do About It*, Aldershot: Gower Publishing Ltd.

■ 48

Force field analysis

■ *How to manage organizational resistance to change*

Force field analysis considers change, from an organizational point of view, in terms of forces for change and forces against change. It regards these forces as being in dynamic equilibrium, a balance which may or may not be conducive to change. Often when managers feel blocked by forces against change, their response is to push harder. This can be counterproductive; the corresponding forces against change can, in turn, increase their response, thus leading to a situation of deadlock. The deadlock can sometimes be between managers and employees. At other times it is simply between those who are for change and those who are against change. The former can be workers and the latter management. Strange but true!

The theory behind the force field analysis is that, rather than increasing the forces for change and possibly incurring the adverse effect noted above, it is very often better to work on reducing the forces against change. In practice, this is much more easily said than done. Very often, however, it is exactly what needs to be done. It is important to realize that reducing the forces against change involves a great deal of negotiation with particular interest groups. This must not be skimped.

How to manage organizational resistance to change using force field analysis

At the directors' workshop which I ran at the beginning of a corporate culture change programme (see 45 Organizational size), certain people's assumptions were becoming increasingly obvious.

'Resistance to change!' snorted Roger Harrison, the production director. 'You'll not get rid of resistance to change. It's human nature.'

'Human nature it may be,' I replied. 'But if we left it at that, we would still be living in caves. The history of the human race is one long story of change. Our primacy over other species is due to our ability to manage change. And managing change means managing resistance to change.'

TABLE 48.1 FORCE FIELD ANALYSIS

Forces For Change	Forces Against Change
Systems organization demands	Pioneer organization thinking/behaviour
Champions of change	Diehards
Market demands for flexibility	Traditional inflexibility
Need for employee participation in securing improvements	Traditional autocratic management
Need to resolve problems rather than merely cope with them	History of secrecy, double dealing
Need to manage change	Incomprehension of how to manage change

---

'Our first effort at a force field analysis (see Table 48.1) shows six forces for change and six corresponding forces against change. Now, from a strictly scientific point of view, one might argue that some of these forces are not forces at all. And one might also argue about whether counter forces were merely reactions. None of this matters. It is best to use force field analysis in a colloquial way rather than a scientific manner.'

'Each force for change is balanced by a force against change. Unless we take heed of these forces against change – which will be felt as resistance to change – then the probability is that we will fail.'

'You won't manage resistance to change by acting macho and stamping on it. We need to realize that resistance arises from perfectly valid reasons. Some of these reasons may have to do with the specific content of change; perhaps something needs to be customized for particular needs. Other reasons may be psychological; people may be hanging their coats on hangers which no longer exist. Whatever the reasons behind forces against change, we need to understand them and be prepared to encounter a wide variety of special interest groups. Ultimately, we want the special interest groups to come into a common fold. But ironically, we won't achieve that unless we firstly recognize their differences. Force field analysis gives us a useful tool. Let's use it!'

Reference
Leigh, A. (1991), *Effective Change. Twenty Ways To Make It Happen*, London: Institute of Personnel Management.

■ 49

Personal culture

■ *How to manage individual*
resistance to change

Most people, whether laypeople or professionals, would
agree that most people are resistant to change. Intriguingly,
the first set of 'most people' is usually deemed to be different
from the second set of 'most people', i.e. it is other people who
are deemed to resist change, not us.

Senior managers, who, perhaps more than most, are aware
of the need for organizational change, often flounder when it
comes to dealing with it. They feel that there are good reasons
for change and deplore the seeming irrationality of their sub-
ordinates.

This approach completely misses the point. Resistance to
change is either due to disagreement with the proposed
change because of rational reasons or because it is psychological. If it is the former, then the disagreement is subject to a
negotiative process; if the latter, treatment is different. Often
supposed rational caveats mask psychological resistance.

We talk about resistence to change as though it were an
essential element of human nature and yet we don't investigate it. This seems silly.

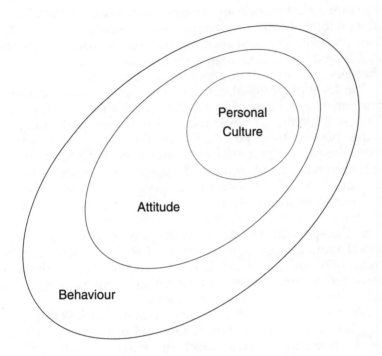

FIGURE 49.1 PERSONAL CULTURE

The model shown in Figure 49.1 suggests that there are three different levels of personal culture, attitude and behaviour. Behaviour is what we do. Attitude is what we assume but are, to some degree, aware of. Personal culture, or psyche, is a much deeper level of personality, norms, belief. Like organizational culture, it is the set of assumptions implicit in behaviour.

As managers, what is ultimately valued is results. To get results, people have to do certain things, in certain ways, i.e. they have to behave. Whatever the rationale for change, whatever the nature of change, ultimately we want people to do things differently, or we want them to do different things or we want a mixture of both. Because attitude and personal culture inhibit behavioural change, managers say, 'he has an attitude problem. We must get him to change his attitude.' This is foolish and misguided. Managers want behaviour and results changing, not attitude or personal culture *per se*.

The level of personal culture corresponds to our identity, our innermost being. For psychological survival, this is a fortress which must never fall. The outer ramparts are attitudes; beyond them lie behaviours. The simple truth is that most people are prepared to change their behaviour, given sufficient reason. But mention of change raises deeper psychological alarms. The notion that personal culture or psyche is threatened immediately invokes the most common of phenomena – resistance to change.

So the approach to take is one of being specific and behavioural about change, to make clear to people that it is not personality or attitude which needs to change, it is results and thus behaviour. People will be given adequate help in a scrupulously blame-free environment.

Most people will find this approach markedly less threatening. It is markedly less threatening and broadly speaking, it works. Ironically, behavioural change will ultimately result in attitudinal change. Eventually our innermost selves will probably also undergo some degree of change – but change on our terms, not someone else's. Our psychological survival will not be threatened. If people's psychological survival is threatened by proposed change, they will strenuously resist it. The converse also holds true.

How to manage individual resistance to change through personal culture

During the directors' workshop which I ran at the beginning of the corporate culture change programme (see 45 Organizational size), arguments about resistance to change were raging.

'So you're saying that if people are not psychologically threatened, there will be far less resistance to change?' Roger, the production director, concluded. 'Precisely,' I replied. 'The catch is, it's easier said than done. We need to make sure that it is done.' 'Quite,' Andrew Kane, the chief executive, drily observed. 'So what do you suggest?' 'Assertiveness.' 'Assertiveness?' 'Yes.'

'You remember that earlier I mentioned assertiveness (see 34 Assertiveness)? Well, I made the point that assertiveness is essential for resolving any issue – not just issues which involve conflict. Obviously when issues do involve conflict, then assertiveness is even more important. But without assertiveness, issues are rarely truly resolved; they are merely coped with. And our job as managers is to be problem resolvers, not problem copers.' At this, Roger nodded thoughtfully.

'One way of regarding change is as conflict – conflict between the past and the future, between people who want to change and those who don't, between people who want this particular change and those who want that particular change. So on this basis, dealing with resistance to change is akin to dealing with conflict. Assertiveness becomes very, very important. Before, it was essential part of the time; now it is essential most of the time.'

'I wondered why you paid so much attention to assertiveness,' Roger ventured. 'Well,' I grinned, 'now you know!'

Reference
Ward, Michael (1994), *Why Your Corporate Culture Change Isn't Working ... And What To Do About It*, Aldershot: Gower Publishing Ltd.

■ 50

The commitment curve

■ *How to achieve successful change*

The commitment curve states that, whatever the rhetoric, in any organization some people will be excited about change and some will dread it. Although it may not be politic for people to reveal their true feelings, there will be a continuum, from those who actively want change to those who equally actively don't want it. One needs to know where people really are on this continuum. The four categories are, in turn:

Actively for change: These are people who are dissatisfied with the *status quo*, perceive the need for change and are willing to make considerable effort to attain such change. They do not merely agree to change; they commit to it, i.e. they actively work at making it happen.

Passively for change: These people may equally accept the rationale for change. However, they are much less willing to pursue it. They agree, rather than commit.

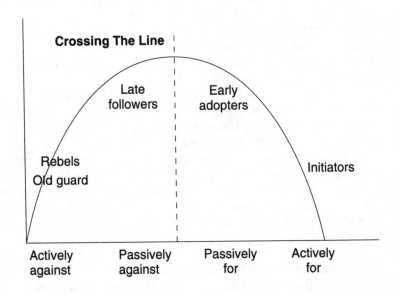

FIGURE 50.1 THE COMMITMENT CURVE

Passively against change: These people do not want change to happen. They may agree to change but their agreement is, in truth, rejection. They cannot be counted upon.

Actively against change: These people know where they stand. They are against change and they are prepared to fight it, if necessary.

How to manage successful change using the commitment curve

At the directors' workshop which I ran at the beginning of a corporate culture change programme (see 45 Organizational size), progress was finally being made.

'Well, I must say this makes perfect sense,' remarked Andrew Kane, the chief executive. 'Some of these models are a bit *outré* for my liking but this one certainly puts people in perspective.' 'I'm not so sure, Andrew,' Roger, the production director, remarked. 'It looks very like the marketing model for consumer reception of new products.'

'In one sense, it is,' I replied. 'That shouldn't surprise us. One might argue that reception of new products would correlate closely with acceptance for change, and demand for new products would similarly correlate with demand for change.'

'You say "change",' Roger protested. 'But we are talking about a whole raft of changes. This isn't a single change that people can accept or reject.' 'That's absolutely true,' I agreed. 'But very often, people's resistance to change is based upon common psychological needs – so the resistance is likely to be widespread.'

'One difference between this curve and the marketing curve is the final category – the rebels and diehards. On the marketing curve, they would be laggards, the very last people who would go out and buy a new product. But, sometimes rebels will go from being actively against change to being actively for change – in a surprisingly short time.' 'If we treat them right?' Andrew Kane put in. 'Precisely,' I agreed. 'Your rebels are your problem people, the ones who don't fit into the organization. In reality, it's the status quo that they are often against, not change, *per se*. Whereas the diehards are truly against change.'

'All of these categories belong to the informal organization,' I continued. 'They are nothing to do with the organization structure.' I looked levelly at all of them. 'I've never yet met a board of directors who began by being actively for change – despite the rhetoric. It is common to have people at board level who are passively, even actively, against change.

'What we have to do is resolve our problems by being honest with ourselves about where we lie on the commitment curve and why we lie there. Once we have put our house in order, it will be time to attend to other people. With ourselves and with others, we must identify where people are, why they are there and what we need to do to gain their commitment. The 'actively fors' will help us most, some of the 'actively againsts' will hinder us most, while others will join the 'actively fors'. Be prepared for surprises! Once we have a majority of power brokers, not necessarily a majority of people, willing to be at least 'passively for' change, then we have reached critical mass – it is then easier for the remainder to come with us than remain against change. Then and only then will we know that we have won.'

It was left to Andrew Kane, the arch pragmatist, to ask, as ever, the pertinent question. 'Will this work?'

'Yes!'

Reference

Ward, Michael (1994), *Why Your Corporate Culture Change Isn't Working ... And What To Do About It*, Aldershot: Gower Publishing Ltd.

Index of techniques